To Al,

a distinguished colleague, mentor
and friend with deep appreciation

Simon Dinitz
October, 1974

Schizophrenics
in the New Custodial Community

Ann E. Davis

Simon Dinitz

Benjamin Pasamanick

Schizophrenics
in the New Custodial Community

Five Years after the Experiment

Ohio State University Press

Copyright © 1974 by the Ohio State University Press
All rights reserved
Manufactured in the United States of America
Cataloging in Publication Data
Davis, Ann, 1932-
    Schizophrenics in the new custodial community.

    Bibliography: p. 193
1. Schizophrenics—Home care.   I.   Dinitz, Simon,
joint author.   II.   Pasamanick, Benjamin, joint author.
III.   Title.
RC514.D28   362.2   74-11383
ISBN 0-8142-0215-2

Contents

Tables

Figures

Foreword

The findings of this longitudinal study and this volume itself have implications far beyond health and mental health, or the causes and treatment of schizophrenia and other mental illnesses. They touch upon all of these, but they throw painful light upon our social sciences, or, more truthfully, on the structures and functions of our social institutions, their goals and directions, and the fundamental choices with which the gatekeepers and members of American society are confronted. In addition to the above, the contents raise a crucial decision for us, the authors, and you, the readers, as to whether the study that preceded the one described in this volume need ever have been done and whether any similar studies should be done at this time.

More direct examination of mental and other public health facilities and of social institutions in some other countries could have told us that their services are instituted earlier and are more efficacious for their beneficiaries than ours. The data available at the time we began the original investigation a dozen years ago were so overwhelming that it is painful to contemplate the fact that we undertook a long, expensive, and arduous study. This follow-up investigation is based on our findings on services in 1964. Given continuing minimal cooperation and financial support, these relatively primitive services would have made some impact upon mental health care in the community in which we did the study; if generalized they probably would have done the same elsewhere.

We are forced to report painful facts in this follow-up volume. The support that might have brought us a bit closer to those qualitatively more advanced countries was not forthcoming. More important, our present governments at almost all levels, and particularly at the highest, have already slashed support for these and most other social services despite what seemed to be firm promises, years of rhetoric, and repeatedly demonstrated need. As a consequence, we are regressing instead of advancing, something that few of us would have believed possible some years ago.

This retrenchment is not unique to the field which we will report upon in this volume. We have merely to mention a few of those in which we have worked over the last two or three decades. One of us has spent years of thought and research in another social institution, criminal justice. The parlous, confused, and viciously harmful activities most governmental judicial agencies have engaged in over the centuries requires no additional comment here.

Another of us has spent more than three decades in an area at least as important, where the evidence is so clear and the facts have such obvious validity that all but a few incomprehensive negativistic individuals would agree with the need for application of the findings. This age-old relationship is between poverty and its concomitants, such as malnutrition, and morbidity, poor growth and abnormal behavioral and nervous system development. Who could seriously question at this time the necessity of an adequate diet for well-being? Nevertheless, studies on behavioral development, of questionable need to begin with, are still being done, sometimes with better design, frequently with poorer, with and without references to some of our research writings and to even older ones.

At this point we must raise questions about the social implications of science, the expenditure of funds and personnel on research whose results are not utilized, and all the personal frustrations of investigators who must feel the tremendous anger of what are, fundamentally, wasted professional lives. Can we continue to spend our time testing programs of service that we know are better performed in other countries? Can we proceed when we are aware that the significant positive findings and the knowledge we have gained will not be put to use? Can we continue to teach our students to enter upon similar lines of research, teaching, or even provision of service to those who need it so badly?

This inquiry is not being written in a spirit of depression or defeatism; it would not have been written at all under such circumstances. However, it is being composed under a cloud of profound unhappiness and pessimism. We are deeply troubled that our society and its institutions may have reached a point of no return. We would offer the Watergate affair as an example on the political level of a basic undermining of the democratic system upon which, at this time in our history, all our social institutions are structured and must depend for their future. This affair must give all of us pause to wonder whether or not some other political approach might serve our society better. Even with all the dangers inherent in social change, a revised system might make it possible to control the hypocrisy, the power-seeking goals, and the destruction of morale and idealism.

In the foregoing we have considered primarily the major macrocosmic social factors that we believe are responsible for the failure to apply our and similar findings to the health problems with which we are confronted. Various writers, particularly public opinion or management surveyors, discuss at great length the microcosmic or intra-institutional variables to which they attribute the neglect of research in changing practice. They blame lack of dissemination of knowledge, claim that no relevant research has been done, or express complete ignorance.

We believe this to be further evidence of the failure of both professionals and consumers to receive adequate education about historical, social, political, and economic factors. Consequently they blame personality and other psychological factors, as well as lack of information, rather than placing the failure with the macrocosmic national sociopolitical institutions where the major causes originate.

Initially, our original longitudinal study received sufficient dissemination so that ignorance could not be claimed. Papers were read at professional societies; a number of papers were published in professional journals; the book *Schizophrenics in the Community*, which reported the findings in detail, received the Hofheimer Prize of the American Psychiatric Association. All of these events were well reported in the lay literature, newspapers, and magazines and were summarized and abstracted for free professional circulation. Indeed, the amount of publicity received became embarrassing, however vain the investigators were. We must repeat that all this publicity played practically no role in altering mental health services in this country. Nevertheless, this book will have served its purpose if it helps to document an empirical study for one area of social functioning and service, what has been described for the country as a whole.

What more can be said to amplify our discussion at the outset of this introduction?

For those readers who still have the stamina and desire to continue with the report for which the preceding was an inevitable jeremiad, we would like to discuss some of the assumptions and clinical impressions, by ourselves and others, relative to the concept of schizophrenia with which we began and ended this study.

We believe that there is a distinct clinical disease entity, schizophrenia, that probably includes most individuals so labeled, plus some others who have escaped such labeling, have been given other labels, or never have been labeled at all. There is considerable evidence to indicate that a relatively large fraction of persons diagnosed as having schizophrenia in this country may very well have affective psychoses, personality disorders, or various chronic organic brain syndromes. This unfortunate lack of diagnostic reliability we believe to be due to gross neglect of clinical instruction and to hypotheses of psychologic determinism that seemed to make it unnecessary to make specific, accurate, or precise diagnoses. There is also considerable evidence that an individual may have more than one illness, complicating the problem of diagnosis and treatment. The work now going on in research centers all over the world, as well as the response to more specific therapy, holds forth considerable hope that reliability of diagnosis is not too far from solution.

We also believe in the overwhelming proportion of cases at this time schizophrenia is in large measure a chronic, lifelong disease. It has remissions and exacerbations that respond, in part, to one or more of the major tranquilizers, permitting individuals to work and lead lives that can be constructive and relatively happy. Remissions occurred before the days of the new drugs but have been helped immeasurably by them. However, we feel certain that the patients included in this study and most of the patients accurately diagnosed as schizophrenic are more or less continuously behaviorally and socially affected.

We believe further that the disease has a recessive hereditary predisposition, although we are not certain whether one or more genes are involved. We also think it possible that some of the heterozygous carriers may exhibit one or more of the enormous complex of primary, secondary, or tertiary symptoms—disturbances in psychological and social perception, various illusions, loss of the capacity to react appropriately emotionally, hallucinations, fear, loneliness, and various disabilities in thinking, such as inability to concentrate, disorganization, fragmentation, irrelevance, and confusion. We think that the best evidence at this time indicates that the enzymatic fault, or faults, involved may lie within the brain or even within certain localized and specific anatomic portions of it.

Some of the case histories we present amply illustrate the manifold nature of the disease. The textbooks of clinical psychiatry and psychology describe the clinical pictures in such great detail that it is unnecessary to do more than refer the reader to ones listed in the bibliography.

We are dealing with one of the major public health problems that seems to have approximately the same prevalence in every country of the world, that is, almost one percent of the population. We have little knowledge of the incidence, since treatment and other confounding variables have made it difficult to determine this, as our study itself indicates. Finally, we must add that schizophrenia is an exceedingly painful and at time destructive disorder in those sick enough to be identified, for the schizophrenic, the family, society generally, and for those who try to care for and treat the patients.

Acknowledgements

It is to the patients, whose lives have been so much a part of ours for several years, that we owe our greatest debt. We have learned from their problems, their failures and their successes. We believe that our efforts have also helped them. To this, we add the hope that this longitudinal research will benefit the many other human beings who suffer and battle schizophrenia.

We wish to acknowledge our great debt to the public health nurses who have worked with us since 1961. These women have been treatment personnel and friends to patients, as well as researchers. Their multiple roles have not always been compatible nor have their efforts been adequately compensated by tangible rewards. We know there is no adequate way to say thank you to Elizabeth Baker, R.N., Raphaelene Kelley, R.N., Mary Jane Raverty, R.N., and Jane A. Waggoner, R.N. It is our sincere hope that the special skills and knowledge you have gained will be recognized, rewarded and, above all, utilized by the mental health agencies for whom you work.

We also owe a considerable debt of gratitude to the administration and personnel of the Kentucky Department of Mental Health. The Kentucky program is one of the best and most progressive in the nation. We know that it takes courage to permit researchers to delve into and evaluate the functioning of a treatment program in this very sensitive area. The systematic faults and treatment problems that we describe in this book are not offered as specific criticisms of the Kentucky system but rather as indicators of the areas in which improvements, across our nation, must be made in the treatment of schizophrenics. Few other state administrators would have cooperated as completely and willingly, donating the time, staff, and facilities we needed to complete this research. Dr. Dale Farabee, then Kentucky Department of Mental Health commissioner, Dr. Ray Hayes, then Central State Hospital superintendent, Dr. David Irigoyen, then Central State Hospital clinical director, and Dr. Cesar Arcangel, then Central Out-patient clinic director made this book possible. We are deeply appreciative.

Dr. William K. Keller, the director of psychiatry at Louisville General Hospital deserves special thanks for his assistance in giving us access to the records of the many patients of ours treated at that hospital. There also were many psychiatrists, clinic directors, social workers, and office personnel whose help was indispensable to us. To all of you—too many to cite each one personally—we extend our appreciation.

Finally the senior author would be remiss if she did not add a very special note of thanks to her husband, Mort, and her sons, Willy and Steve. There is no way to repay the sacrifices you have made by giving me the opportunity to complete my research and this book.

Preface

In this preface we believe it may be of value to locate our work, and interpret its relevance with respect to the broader social and psychiatric organizational issues of our times. In so doing we shall offer our views about the current status of community mental health centers, the state mental hospitals, and the effectiveness of these delivery systems for the care of schizophrenics. The foci we believe to be most relevant for effective care will be presented, especially when they may be lacking or poorly conceived within our present system.

The Current Status of Community Mental Health

"No one is interested in community mental health any more"; such a comment was made recently at a mental health conference. Although more extreme in tone than sentiments expressed by most people, this view mirrors a growing disenchantment with the dream born in the mid-1950s and nurtured by the Federal Mental Health Act. The spirit of the last decade with unbridled optimism in regard to the new millennium in mental health was made possible by the obvious success of the medications for patients, reports of successes with milieu therapy in the hospital, and with an impetus in the form of federal funds for the building and later staffing of the regional mental health centers. Practitioners believed that a new era had arrived whereupon the state hospitals were to become archaic and irrelevant and would be replaced by new centers for mental health care, accessible to the people, that would provide a variety of flexible services for a wide range of emotionally related difficulties. The envisioned community-care utopia was initiated and found lacking. It is not the conception that has proven improbable but human beings, their functioning and modes of organization. Many people most recently dismayed by the cut backs in federal money for mental health endeavors, and by the continuance of fallible care systems which persist in the face of better technical knowledge, are withdrawing and expressing a new found apathy toward community mental health.

It is interesting that an ideology could ever have made much of a difference, for in reality the delivery of care has never changed much. What needs to be done, at least for schizophrenics, is in fact very simple and available regardless of whether the approach is in-community, in-hospital, milieu, or any other. The custodial hospital has meanwhile died a natural and inevitable death with the advent of medications in the care of psychoses and there is no reason to expect it can ever be resurrected; for this we are all grateful.

The Community Mental Health Center

What is the status of the dream of community mental health care for the schizophrenic? There has been very little systematic study of, but a sizable degree of debate about, the actual functioning of the community centers. Let us take the time to comment on some of the literature concerning the ineffectiveness of such centers with psychotics and schizophrenics. Michael Gorman says that the centers are a failure, they are an extension of private psychiatry that treats the upper-income neurotics who have Blue Cross coverage.[1] A similar complaint is voiced by George Albee who says that the centers fail because they are housed in, or are adjacent to, general hospitals where fees are charged; therefore the poor patients and many of the severely disturbed who can not pay are not treated in the community.[2] Private psychiatry, Albee charges, refuses to meet the public need. Such allegations do in fact appear supported by the statis-

1. Michael Gorman, "The Public Arena, pp. 299–302.
2. George Albee, "Through the Looking Glass," pp. 293–98.

tics for the current year in the state of Indiana. By diagnostic categories it is possible to see that the community clinics treat primarily neurotics and others with similar diagnostic problems; this is much in contrast to the state mental hospitals where diagnosable psychotics and schizophrenics far outnumber others. Systematic research on the question needs to be conducted, but from personal experience along with the above information the failure of community clinics to assume state hospital burdens appears to be true.

Why should this situation exist when the rationale for the creation of mental health centers was explicitly to initiate the demise of state custodial institutions by providing this alternative system; and also why, when there is ample research evidence to show that psychotics can be treated effectively in the community? For such proof we refer to our original *Schizophrenics in the Community* study.[3] Also, Englehardt and Freedman found in their seven years of research (even though their patients were primarily ambulatory schizophrenics) that they could be treated quite successfully in the community with medications.[4]

Why, then, have psychotics remained on the wards of in-hospital programs? Lawrence Kolb attempts an answer when he says it is not clear to the public that community mental health clinics are intended for people with severe psychoses. Additional difficulties of the center he says are: (1) that there are not enough psychiatrists available to staff all of the proposed "full range of service" clinics; (2) that regional clinics are not coordinated with welfare and other community services, thus hindering their ability to provide care for the lower-class population; (3) that clinics threaten both state hospital personnel as well as private psychiatrists either on the level of job security or as evidence of actualized trends toward socialized medicine; and (4) that the possibility exists that psychiatrists are not trained to provide the community leadership for these facilities.[5]

Some of Dr. Kolb's statements are more true than others. To us the organizational problems appear to be the most important. Mental health clinics are variously located and variously staffed; at times they are situated in general medical hospitals and at times in the

3. Benjamin Pasamanick, Frank Scarpitti, and Simon Dinitz, *Schizophrenics in the Community: An Experimental Study in the Prevention of Hospitalization*.

4. David M. Englehardt and Norbert Freedman, "Maintenance Drug Therapy: The Schizophrenic in the Community," pp. 256–82.

5. Lawrence C. Kolb, M.D., "Community Mental Health Centers," pp. 283–93.

basements of old welfare buildings. Some of the new clinics are exhaustive and fine facilities with a full range of services. Such a center must have psychiatrists and in-patient beds, and if it does, it competes with the existing private facilities and also directly threatens the functions of the state mental hospitals. It is to such complete centers that one would anticipate the maximum of resistance from both the private and public traditional care sectors. The smaller, lesser staffed and equipped clinics also have difficulties but for other reasons; such a clinic lacks the manpower, medical supervision, and facilities to cope with psychotics. At the worst, believing they lack the above, the small clinic defers handling these so-called harder cases to the existing hospital facility. Furthermore, from the viewpoint of the public, the lower-class family has historically gone to the courts, the police, and the city general hospital emergency room in the midst of a serious crisis with the disturbed family member; once such machinery is started the patient is already disposed of as "serious" in the state facility. The reeducation process is a sizable one given the social class, the tradition, and the emergency appearance of these schizophrenics' hospital admissions. Cooperative rerouting to community centers necessitates strong mandates to families and existing agencies of nonadmittance or emergency acceptance in the traditional mode, and such refusals are difficult to give; crises, low educational levels, and legalities all converge to perpetuate the old system. Little has thus far been said about domains, power, economics, and interagency communications. The community mental health clinic is a voluntary enterprise, and the expectation that more traditional facilities will freely yield financial or territorial holdings, political powers, or even acquiesce to new community expertise with grace is undoubtedly a myth. We have encountered this problem in our society in other social and political arenas; a lesson that for some reason we fail to internalize, face, and fully anticipate.

The State Mental Hospital

If in fact the community mental health centers are not fulfilling their functions, what of the state mental hospitals? In a fairly recent study Mandelbrote and Trick find that 41 percent of the chronic schizophrenics admitted to a state hospital are discharged and readmitted within a two-year period; and an additional 13 percent remain in the hospital for the duration of the two-year period; the remaining 46 percent of the patients are not readmitted.[6] When the follow-up period is extended to five years (as in our study) an average of 60 percent of the patients experience rehospitalizations. These statistics indicate that we have created a revolving-door system to replace the custodial hospital; such facts cloud the enthusiastic statements that are made by proponents of the new hospital philosophy and of its reduced hospital population.

Bertram S. Brown, director of the National Institute of Mental Health, in an address before the Tennessee Legislature in March of 1973 stated, "In the mid 1950s state mental hospitals had a population just under 600,000. Just 15 years later we have achieved the goal of cutting that number by 50 percent—there are now fewer than 300,000 patients in institutions for the mentally ill in the United States. The difference between that figure and the 800,000 or 900,-000 that we estimated would be there had the trend not been reversed, represents billions of dollars of expenditures whose savings I am sure you can appreciate."[7]

To take issue with Dr. Brown's position, it can be said that although we have reduced the resident populations of our state facilities we have done so by rotating a higher volume of patients, via readmission, through the facilities. Although patients no longer remain for lifetimes or partial lifetimes, the majority of patients face repeated community, social, and psychiatric failures that require readmission to these hospitals. Also on Dr. Brown's second point it is necessary to offer a refinement and clarification of the savings of billions of dollars by the reduction of in-patient resident populations. Our data show that the majority of patients do not hold jobs nor do they function very well in their domestic roles; most patients ultimately alienate their families and are divorced or rejected by their primary groups. In short, most patients are dependent members of society, and many are recipients of welfare grants based on mental disability. Of the elderly that are discharged from the state facilities, the majority are transfered to nursing or boarding homes to be therein supported by welfare or public monies of some sort; in no sense have the majority of discharged schizophrenics become con-

6. B. M. Mandelbrote and K. L. K. Trick, "Social and Clinical Factors in the Outcome of Schizophrenia," pp. 24–34.

7. Bertram S. Brown, M.D., Address presented in Nashville, Tennessee, 6 March 1973.

tributing members of society; they continue to cost America billions of dollars, but the money is now less visibly dispersed by other public agencies. The state mental hospitals, statistically, appear to be doing a good job, but when viewed at close range the flaws in their success become evident. Our purpose herein is not to chastise these facilities but to probe them and arouse administrators and practitioners to that which is within their grasp, the provision of effective services to schizophrenics.

Our current system is a dual one, much as it has been throughout America's history; there is one care system for the public sector and yet another for private patients. Given our heritage this dichotomy is likely to continue for some time, and in terms of the actualities of care for schizophrenics it does not really matter. The point is that both systems often fail with schizophrenics whereas both could fairly well succeed. It does not matter whether the appropriate care is given in the hospital or outside of it, or by private or public psychiatry. What does matter is that the treatment is correct and directed toward the basic requirements of patient care, a point to which we now address ourselves.

Needs of Schizophrenics

The basic needs of schizophrenic patients are three: (1) medication; (2) socio-supportive attention to their families; and (3) the provision of the minimum necessities of life for the patients, such as food, medical attention, housing, and an opportunity to meaningfully occupy their time. Let us survey these needs one at a time.

Medications

Although there are subtleties yet to be resolved, in the last decade the overwhelming research evidence has shown the necessity for using medications in treating schizophrenics. The only debate that remains concerns the ambulatory schizophrenic. This is a patient who has no hospital history and has maintained a marginal community adjustment. Our original home-care study shows that, although drugs prevent hospitalizations among the ambulatory group more than treatment with placebos, the evidence is far less convincing than for similar comparisons on already hospitalized schizophrenics. Englehardt and Freedman, in their study on long-term maintenance of outpatient schizophrenics, caution that drugs may have an adverse effect on non-hospital-prone patients.[8] We suspect that the effect of the medication on ambulatory patients may not be so much adverse as it is ineffective.

The hospital-prone schizophrenic should be distinguished from ambulatory non-hospital-prone patients. The hospital-prone patients, upon reviewing our findings and those of others, can be identified by the following characteristics: (1) social isolation along with a pre-morbid withdrawal such as asocial behavior and a lack of interest in one's peers; (2) low socioeconomic status, low occupational status, and little education; and (3) a negligible or absent previous hospital history along with a short-term illness. Fourth, a summary of the literature indicates that a patient's symptoms are a poorer prognostic device than the patient's previous history and the extent to which he has been able to be successfully involved in social life.[9] If a physician is uncertain about the hospital proneness of his patient, in our judgement, it would be best to err on the side of using medications.

It is conversely mandatory that the hospital-prone and chronic schizophrenic be treated continuously with medications, in a stable setting, over a long period of time, possibly for the duration of his lifetime. Englehardt reports that drugs used over a long period of time are well tolerated and are free of serious toxicity.[10] Caffey, et al., report, "Long term uninterrupted medication (over 10 years) has proved feasible so that one should not feel impelled to discontinue the drug except in the presence of a side effect of overriding importance."[11] These authors also add that the minimal dose at which a patient functions best is the most feasible; furthermore, clinical addiction is unknown and it is virtually impossible to commit suicide with these medications as the sole agent. Winkelman, in yet another

8. Englehardt and Freedman, "Maintenance Drug Therapy," pp. 256–82.

9. The reader is referred to the works of: Englehardt and Freedman, "Maintenance Drug Therapy," pp. 256–82 (on items 1, 2, and 4); Rachel Gittleman-Klein and Donald F. Klein, "Premorbid Asocial Adjustment and Prognosis in Schizophrenia," pp. 35–53 (on item 1); Martin Harrow, Gary J. Tucker, and Evelyn Bromet, "Short Term Prognosis of Schizophrenic Patients," pp. 195–202 (on items 1, 2, 3, and 4); K. Flekkøy, C. Astrup, and T. Hartmann, "Word Association in Schizophrenics: A Ten-Year Follow up," pp. 209–16 (on item 2); B. M. Mandelbrote and K. L. K. Trick, "Social and Clinical Factors in the Outcome of Schizophrenia," pp. 24–34 (on item 3).

10. Englehardt and Freedman, "Maintenance Drug Therapy," pp. 256–82.

11. Eugene M. Caffey Jr., M.D., Leo H. Hollister, M.D., Samuel C. Kaim, M.D., Alex D. Pokorny, M.D., "Drug Treatment in Psychiatry," pp. 428–71.

study, finds that with patients on medication for over ten and one-half years discontinued or partial doses are less effective than continued and full medication.[12]

The medications have been found to be most effective early in the patient's illness and their corrective value appears to diminish over time, yet discontinuance risks the recurrence of psychotic symptoms and the initiation of a rehospitalization. It appears evident that many practitioners fail because they neglect to maintain schizophrenics on their medications. Reasons for such failures are based on: (1) erroneous assumptions that the patient's improvement warrants discontinuance of medication; (2) the breakdown in referrals from hospital to after-care clinics; (3) the lack of education given to families regarding the need for continued medication and after care for the patient; and (4) the absence of aggressive follow-up for patients who fail voluntarily to keep after-care clinic appointments. None of these four faults is beyond correction if the importance of what is being said reaches the psychiatric personnel treating schizophrenics.

Family Support

The second need of the schizophrenic population is for family support. What is meant by this is not formal family psychotherapy, but family education regarding the necessity for after care and medications for the patient, the provision of qualified personnel who can listen to family members' problems with the patient and offer common-sense suggestions while providing emotional support, and lastly the offering of social service referrals for the whole family to assure that the entire range of community resources is available and used by the multi-problemed family. Social service referrals should include such help as vocational guidance, financial aid, medical care, and recreational needs.

Despite numerous references in the literature to both family therapy with neurotics as well as research studies on therapy with families of schizophrenics, very little is actually done in the field with families. Hospitals focus on the patient and contact families only at admission and discharge; ironically, hospital personnel often hold a negative attitude toward families who they believe dump and abandon patients at the hospital. Outpatient clinics are also guilty of simi-

12. N. M. Winkelman, Jr., "A Clinical and Sociocultural Study of 200 Psychiatric Patients Started on Chloropromazine 10 1/2 Years Ago," pp. 861–69.

lar omissions. Occasionally clinic personnel see key members of the family, but, failing to do so regularly, the extent of the patient's problem behavior at home remains unknown to the clinic staff.

The evidence of need for family-oriented support is not purposively and clearly presented in the research literature. Our study is one of the few to show that added percentages of patients are saved from hospitalization when family-focused services are added to the typical outpatient care. Mandelbrote and Trick state, as we, that simply because a patient is discharged from the hospital it ought not be expected that psychiatric and social problems have been solved. Mandelbrote says that 20 percent of the patients in their study who managed to avoid rehospitalization had persistent symptoms and psychotic episodes and were burdens in the community.[13] Our data on problem behavior of patients in the home implies that even higher percentages than the above are problematic in their homes.

Englehardt and Freedman, in their work on outpatient clinic care of schizophrenics, found that, in the course of their work, they lost 61 percent of their out patients by the end of the first 12 months of their study.[14] To the best of our knowledge these researchers did not pursue patients who failed to keep their clinic appointments; further, they did not work with families or offer any social-work intervention to the family. The researchers concluded that in addition to medication patients need other kinds of care (which they do not specify) to prevent hospitalization over a long period of time. We posit that, in light of our findings, what is missing is work with the family, an ingredient we have found to be very beneficial in the treatment of schizophrenics.

Basic Life Needs of Patients

Previously in the discussion on hospital-prone patients we noted that patients with low socioeconomic status, little education, and social isolationist tendencies comprise the poorer risks. It is our belief that these are the very areas (plus general medical care) in which patients need continual support. Although our data gives us little cause to be optimistic about our abilities to slow down a tendency for patients to deteriorate over time in their vocational, domes-

13. B. M. Mandelbrote and K. L. K. Trick, "Social and Clinical Factors in Schizophrenia," pp. 24–34.
14. Englehardt and Freedman, "Maintenance Drug Therapy," pp. 256–82.

tic, or marital adjustments, it is also evident that these social areas need further research and practical attention. It is currently much easier to contain the psychotic and disturbed mental productions óf the patient than it is to effect positive social adaptations; also, psychiatric states are not clearly correlated with good socio-adaptive abilities. Yet, our case histories provide evidence on some patients in which positive cycles of social competence are initiated, and we therefore believe that it is possible to achieve better social adjustments for patients and that we must focus on this area as ʼour next level of challenge in the case of schizophrenics.

We have arrived full cycle in our commentary on the basic requirements for good patient care. The areas we have outlined are medications, family support, and provisions for the patient's basic human needs. We have found that these are often neglected in patient care, and we offer our volume as evidence in support of this perspective. The reader may note in this book the time periods in which such basic services were lacking and the consequences of this for the patients.

Schizophrenics
in the New Custodial Community

chapter one

Introduction: Origins of the Study

This volume presents the results of seven years of research information on 152 schizophrenic patients with whom study began in a home
care experiment in Louisville, Kentucky; this original study started
in 1961 and ended in 1964. A book presenting the results of that project entitled, *Schizophrenics in the Community: An Experimental
Study in the Prevention of Hospitalization*, was published in 1967.
The original experiment constitutes the basis for our follow-up;
therefore we shall begin with a brief review of the methods and
findings of that first study.

The specific objective of the experiment in 1961 was to demonstrate that actively psychotic patients could be treated in their homes
as successfully, if not more successfully, as in hospital facilities.
Furthermore, not only could schizophrenics be treated at home,
thereby averting hospitalization, but such care could be accomplished with a minimum of psychiatric and professional personnel
or facilities. The design called for treatment that consisted primarily of home visitations by public health nurses who dispensed tranquilizing drugs prescribed by a project psychiatrist who supervised
medications and held office consultations at prescribed intervals with
patients.

The sample provided for the inclusion of a control group of patients. To insure that subjects selected were acutely psychotic schizophrenics, patients were taken from two hospitals shortly after their

admissions and were, after screening, sent back home to their families under the care of the experimental study staff. The study clinic was called the Institute Treatment Center and was affiliated with the Kentucky Department of Mental Health.[1]

To qualify for acceptance into the project each patient had to meet these criteria: (1) have a diagnosis of schizophrenia, (2) be neither homicidal nor suicidal, (3) be between the ages of 18 and 60, (4) reside in the city of Louisville or in an adjacent county, and (5) have a family that would accept him while providing supervision in the home.

If a patient met the above conditions he was randomly assigned to one of three study groups: one group (the home care drug group, 40 percent of the sample) was sent home on drugs under ITC care; a second, the home care placebo group (30 percent of the sample), was sent home on placebo medication; and a third group, the controls (30 percent of the sample), was returned to the hospital to undergo the usual course of hospital care. With this distribution it became possible for the researchers to compare the success of patients maintained on drugs at home and visited by the nurses with patients at home on placebos who were also visited by nurses; they could also compare both groups with a control group of patients processed through the usual course of hospital care in the public mental hospital system.

Patients for the study came from three sources, the regional state mental hospital, the psychiatric unit of the city general hospital, and from general practitioners in the community. Problems encountered with patients sent by the general practitioners occurred when patients living in the community resisted going to a hospital despite the fact that they needed hospitalization and their illnesses were deemed comparable to the disorders of already hospitalized patients. Since these patients rejected hospitalization when their sample selection indicated they were to become part of the hospital control group it was necessary to separate them from the rest of the patients, thereby creating a fourth category, "ambulatory home care group." They also were randomly assigned either to home care on drugs or home care on placebos, but no further attempts were made to send them to a hospital as part of a control group.

1. The study and the research center will hereafter be referred to by the abbreviation ITC.

The Original Experimental Program:
Staff and Project Procedure

The ITC experimental staff consisted of a sociologist as director, a part-time psychiatrist, a psychologist, a social worker, and five nurses with public health nursing experience; only one of the nurses had a background in psychiatric nursing. The functions of the staff were to provide treatment to patients and, systematically, to collect research data. The psychiatrist, upon receipt of a new referral, confirmed the diagnosis of schizophrenia made by the hospital physician and became solely responsible for the prescription of drugs even though he was unaware of whether the prescription, filled by the research director, contained active medications or a placebo. Completing two psychiatric rating forms that provided standarized measures of the patient's psychiatric status, he personally saw patients at intake, at six months, and at twenty-four months after their acceptance into the study.

The social worker received the names of referred patients from the hospitals, after which she made the initial contact with families to judge if they could meet the criteria for home care, in particular, the supervision of the patient. Very few families capable of supervising the patient refused the prospect of ITC home care; in fact families of patients selected as hospital controls were disappointed when the patient was not allowed to go home under the ITC staff's care. The social worker, aside from assisting in the sample selection, took an initial social history inventory covering social, economic, and treatment aspects of the patient's background. As practicing clinicians the psychiatrist as well as the social worker served as consultants and advisers to the public health nurses who were charged with the main burden of patient and family home contacts.[2]

The psychologist's responsibility consisted of the administration of a battery of psychological tests providing a sequential inventory of the patient's psychological status, emotional health, aptitudes, and I.Q. These tests were given to the entire study population at intake and at regular intervals thereafter.

Every patient accepted for home care was assigned to a nurse who visited him weekly at first, later biweekly, and then less frequently

2. For a description of the role of the project social worker see Joseph Albini, "The Role of the Social Worker in an Experimental Community Mental Health Clinic: Experiences and Future Implications," pp. 111–19.

following a preset schedule of visitations that was followed regardless of the patient's condition. The nurse on each visit to the patient's home took a supply of medication and talked with the patient as well as with a significant other.[3] The nurse completed numerous research forms dealing with the patient's symptom manifestations, social behavior, attitudes, and task performances. After each visit she wrote a narrative report for the psychiatrist, which enabled him to evaluate the patient's psychiatric and social adjustment in the community. Patients in the hospital control group were also brought to the clinic to be evaluated at regular intervals.

If a home care patient became so unmanageable that he could not remain in the community, hospitalization was recommended by the psychiatrist and he was judged a project failure. In addition failures occurred when the patient moved away from the treatment locale, or when he or the family withdrew from the treatment program by refusing to cooperate; some occurred when the home situations changed and hospitalization became necessary to provide supervision for the patient.

In all, 226 patients were involved in the project; of these, the 57 drug home care, 41 placebo home care, and 54 hospital controls were followed for a period ranging from nine months to thirty months. There were also 36 privately referred ambulatory home care patients on drugs and 27 ambulatory home care patients on placebos. By the time the project had terminated 11 cases were failures because of noncooperation from the family or the patient; they were termed dropouts. Although not substantially different from the study population on demographic characteristics the dropouts are not included in the study findings that follow.

Findings of the Original Study

1. Over 77 percent of the state hospital referred home care drug patients, but only 34 percent of the placebo home care cases, remained at home throughout their entire project time. All controls, of course, were hospitalized and were at least initially treated in the hospitals. The major finding was that acutely psychotic patients could be cared for at home and, if on drugs, successfully.[4]

3. The significant other, henceforth called the SO, was the most important member of the household, in relational terms, to the patient and was usually a spouse or parent.

4. Pasamanick, Scarpitti, and Dinitz, *Schizophrenics in the Community*. See Chapter 4 of this book for a detailed summary of the listed study findings.

2. Successful home care patients not only remained out of the hospital but also showed improvement in mental status, psychological test performance, domestic functioning, and social participation scores. These gains were substantial and some were statistically significant. On all of the many specific measures, home care patients were functioning as well as or better than the hospital control cases who had received the usual care given to a hospitalized patient.

3. Patients who failed and had to be hospitalized usually did so soon after their acceptance into the program; nearly all failures occurred within six months of study intake.

4. Hospital controls, once discharged and after presumable remission of their grosser symptoms, failed more often at home than did ITC home care patients.

5. Failure in home care was of the "last straw" variety; the patients' behavior had become so bizarre or dangerous as to be intolerable, and the responsible relatives could no longer cope with the situation.

6. Most of the improvement in patients' domestic, social, and psychiatric performance occurred in the first six months of the study. Thereafter functioning improved very little, if at all. Once the acute signs and symptoms abated functioning usually returned to a pre-episodic level; thereafter there were few gains.

7. Of the general practitioners' community-referred drug and placebo patients (the ambulatory cases) nearly 76 percent of the drug and 61 percent of the placebo cases succeeded on home care. In instances of hospitalization failures occurred early and the precipitants were generally like those for hospital-referred patients who failed.

8. After treatment, and at their very best, all categories of patients continued to have considerable difficulty in adequate role performance and in coping with their psychological symptoms.

The ITC project was able to demonstrate that actively psychotic schizophrenics, given the use of drugs, could be cared for in their own homes; further that such care was as effective as hospital care when measured in terms of the patients' psychiatric statuses, psychological functioning, social behavior, or vocational behavior. Home care had the distinct advantage of circumventing the stigma of hospitalization and the concomitant social and emotional trauma resulting from prolonged separation from family and community.

The project ended in 1964 and the ITC home care patients were referred to other available community treatment agencies; in each patients' case referrals were made to facilities believed best suited to the patient's treatment and aftercare needs. Most cases were transferred to the outpatient care clinics of the state hospital system; the second largest group was sent to the outpatient clinic at the local general hospital.

Since then, to the best of our knowledge, no similar home care program has been initiated either as a research project or as an ongoing treatment facility anywhere in the United States. The interested reader is referred to an article by Simon Dinitz that analyzes the lack of practical impact this project had despite acclaim it received from the psychiatric community.[5]

Theoretical Problems in Follow-up Studies

Follow-up studies on mental patients have been rarer than those dealing with theoretical considerations, case studies, treatment programs, or the etiology of mental disorders. Studies may be divided into those that deal with treatment experiments and include evaluations of their outcomes and those studies that simply assess the adjustments of patients after they have completed a course of treatment. The latter, most simply, may be categorized as follow-up studies. Among such studies we will examine the works of the following people: Shirley Angrist, Simon Dinitz, Howard Freeman, August Hollingshead, William Michaux, Dorothy Miller, Lois Molholm, Jerome Myers, and Benjamin Pasamanick.[6]

Studies and their content should be conceptualized categorically to help clarify the nature of the research findings. For instance, studies may deal with one sex, or with both, but given the importance of physiological differences (witness psychoses precipitated by menopause) and the differences in life style and social roles peculiar to each sex, a description and an awareness of a study's sex composition is important.

5. Simon Dinitz, "Policy Implications of an Experimental Study in the Home Care of Schizophrenics," pp. 1–20.

6. Shirley Angrist et al., *Women After Treatment: A Study of Former Mental Patients and Their Normal Neighbors*; Howard E. Freeman and Ozzie G. Simmons, *The Mental Patient Comes Home*; William Michaux et al., *The First Year Out: Mental Patients After Hospitalization*; Dorothy Miller, *Worlds That Fail: Part I: Retrospective Analyses of Mental Patients*; Lois Molholm, "Female Patients and Normal Female Controls: A Restudy Ten Years Later"; Jerome K. Myers and Lee L. Bean, *A Decade Later: A Follow-up of Social Class and Mental Illness*.

Differences in studies also exist on the diagnostic types of the patients included in a sample. For a long time theoreticians believed that neuroses, functional psychoses (those with no known physical cause), and organically based psychoses (those with an apparent physical basis) were sufficiently different disorders to merit separate classifications and differential treatment. Since Dunham's study on the variable distributions of mental disorders by urban areas, substantial support for the clinical belief that manic depression and schizophrenia are different disorders has been available.[7] Since Hollingshead's study it has also been known that neuroses and psychoses occur differentially among the social classes and that treatment practices differ correspondingly.[8] Too frequently research is conducted as though all mentally ill form a single category or population with a unitary disorder called *mental illness*. Whenever possible a researcher must strive to separate his study populations by diagnoses to avoid obscuring important findings.

Another way in which studies vary and make the comparison of results difficult is by the selection of sample populations from different treatment agencies. Samples may be drawn from private psychiatric practices, clinics, or hospitals that provide private care, or from state hospitals and clinics, or federal agencies. Different social classes with different life styles, and illnesses, are the recipients of differing types and degrees of care. This area is another in which caution needs to be exercised in evaluating the researcher's sample selection and data analysis.

A major factor of concern in comparing follow-up research is the time span over which patients' adjustments are studied. Results of studies have been reported for as brief a period as one month after release from treatment to as long as ten years later. At the risk of sounding trite, let it be said if a long enough time span is included in a study the majority of the patients (modified by the nature of the disorder and a few other variables) will become treatment failures. Researchers, and readers of the literature alike, need to exercise caution when comparing results from studies covering widely divergent time spans.

With this brief review of theoretical and practical problems, let

7. H. Warren Dunham and Robert E. Faris, *Mental Disorders in Urban Areas.*

8. August B. Hollingshead and Fredrick C. Redlich, *Social Class and Mental Illness.*

us look at the composition of major follow-up studies that relate to the study we have conducted. The Dinitz and Angrist sample consists only of women; includes all types of diagnostic disorders, and draws its patients from a select university-hospital population; the follow-up period is approximately two years in length. The Freeman and Simmons work includes both men and women, of all diagnostic types, drawn from a state-hospital population; it covers only a single year of follow-up time. Myers and Bean deal with males and females selected from public-care facilities and include all diagnostic categories. Their patients were treated in both clinics and hospitals; the study covers a ten-year period. A drawback of Myers and Bean's work is their almost exclusive concern with socioeconomic status as an explanatory variable for patients' adjustments.

The reader will note that none of these studies deals exclusively with a homogeneous diagnostic population such as the schizophrenics in the ITC study, or are followed for as long a period (five years), or have selected patients exclusively from public facilities. Of added interest is the fact that patients in our study were known personally and in depth by the researchers. Also of concern is the fact that the loss rate of patients for which no information was collected amounted to only 8 percent in our follow-up.

Judging Patients as Successes

The next area with which evaluators must be concerned is the criteria used for adjudging patients as successes or failures. To date, studies have dealt with a wide variety of variables and have correlated them with post-hospital role, task performance, or failure and success as measured by rehospitalization. Early studies made the assumption that the quality of task and role performance was linked to mental status and almost surely with success or failure as measured by rehospitalization.

Much of the basis for the entry of sociology into research in mental disorder rested on ideas concerning the influence of social environment, role demands, and social expectations—in essence, social structure—upon patient behavior. Sociologists sought to shed light on the etiology of mental disorders and on the lessening or exacerbation of psychiatric symptoms, the latter thought to be caused or at least aggravated by social factors. A sociological emphasis, in the extreme, may be viewed in the writing of Thomas Szasz whose labeling approach viewed social structure and especially the authority structure as the noxious causative element in mental disorder.[9]

Rudimentary elements of doubt crept into sociological work as studies in the 1950s of Dinitz and his colleagues, and then the works of Simmons and Freeman, arrived at the surprising conclusion that social structural factors and intrapsychic factors were to be considered as separate elements in the determination of patient performance. They suggested that patients although good social performers—task adequate—could not be distinguished in some cases from the normal, they could still be hospital failures in need of psychiatric treatment. Conversely, poor task performers were, in fact, often psychiatrically well. Simmons and Freeman found it necessary to separate the question of success as judged by social or role performance standards and success as measured by avoidance of rehospitalization.

Recent research is confronted with the fact that demands for psychiatric intervention arise due to impaired psychiatric functioning, malfunctions of cognitive and emotive mental capacities, in essence as due to intrapsychic phenomena less than as responses to social behaviors such as isolation, poor domestic performance, poor job performance, or economic dependency. In this follow-up, care shall be continually taken to alert the reader regarding the criteria used to measure adjustment or success.

The part that economic security or social class plays in psychiatric failure remains unclear. Undoubtedly at the gross level of analysis, upper- versus lower-class status, more psychoses occur in the lower-class ranks and more of the patients remain in quasi-custodial or drug-treatment oriented facilities.[10] Despite this broad differentiation, when explanations within social classes are desired, economic factors fail to distinguish between hospital returnees and nonreturnees. Nonetheless, economic variables occupy an important position in the forthcoming analyses.

In this study uses are made of social-structural and other social variables such as marital status, domestic performance, and vocational performance, as well as psychiatric variables, mental status reports, and problem behavior checklists. It is hoped that this eclectic approach may permit a clarification of the nature of the factors responsible for hospital returns.

9. Thomas S. Szasz, "The Myth of Mental Illness," pp. 113–18.
10. Hollingshead and Redlich, *Social Class and Mental Illness.*

Objectives of the Follow-up

This report, because of the size of the follow-up, must of necessity deal with only a portion of the collected data. Under examination is the possibility of demonstrating that a population of schizophrenics may need continued treatment supervision and that without such after care their recovery experiences are often less than satisfactory.

An objective of our follow-up is to determine the adaptive abilities of patients in various treatment categories, as measured by the times they were rehospitalized and by the length of time spent in the hospital. At follow-up the patients' levels of functioning in the community in vocational, social, and domestic areas, and in problem behavior are examined. This broad evaluative base, by comparing the three study groups, home drug care, placebo, and control, permits a determination of whether ITC home care had a lasting or diminishing effect over the years.

Another aim of the analyses is a longitudinal view of the ability of schizophrenics to adjust in the community. A long-term perspective is valuable in clarifying the question of whether schizophrenia is a chronic and disabling illness that limits patients' abilities to cope with life-survival demands.

A final objective is an examination of familial reactions to differing types of deviant behavior and psychopathology as correlates of rehospitalization. This objective is pursued by examining familial living situations and the patients' behavior within the family group.

Building upon prior research, this study may assist in answering the question of why certain patients are rehospitalized and others, seemingly equally ill, remain at home. We have recognized the fact that rehospitalized patients are not necessarily those with the poorest task and social performances. A clarification of such questions occupies a large measure of the follow-up study efforts.

Hypotheses and General Methodology

The follow-up was conducted with the complete cooperation of the Kentucky Department of Mental Health. This assistance included access to all hospital and clinic records and the use of other necessary facilities. Fortunately all original ITC study nurses, with one exception, were available to serve as interviewers and to help in other phases of data collection. Since the termination of the original study the nurses had been employed by the Kentucky Department of Mental Health and in most cases they had maintained contact with the ITC patients over the years. In this follow-up the nurses interviewed their previous ITC home care patients, with few exceptions.

The interview schedule was, in most essentials, identical with the original ITC instruments; items were re-used to permit comparability between the former study and the follow-up research. Chapter two describes data collection methods in detail and difficulties encountered in our work.

At follow-up the patient's significant other, the SO, was interviewed to obtain the vast majority of the follow-up data. Each patient was informally interviewed, giving the nurse an opportunity to note change in behavior, appearance, or personality over the years since the original study. Interviews took place in the patients' homes or in the hospital if the patient was hospitalized. To supplement the home interviews, hospital and clinic records covering a five-year period on all the patients from every treatment facility in the area were reviewed for corroborative and supplementary information.

Hypothesis One

There will be no significant differences between the home care and the hospital control groups in frequency of rehospitalizations and days spent in the hospital since the termination of the ITC program. (In essence we believe that withdrawal of the ITC home care resulted in a declining patient adjustment for the home care group.)

The test of this hypothesis depends upon a count of the total days of hospitalization for each of the three project groups from the termination of the original ITC project to the beginning of the follow-up. This information is analyzed by comparing the numbers of rehospitalizations and the mean number of days per hospital stay within each study group. To provide added perspectives on the patients' treatment experiences, the clinic care history of each patient is studied from the end of the original ITC study in 1964 to the follow-up in 1969.

Hypothesis Two

There will be no significant differences between the home care and the control groups in their current levels of functioning on vocational, social, domestic, marital, or psychological variables. (Again, the assumption is that the advantaged home study group regressed to the lesser adjustment levels of other patients after ITC home care was withdrawn.)

The test of this hypothesis depends upon the collection of data on vocational, domestic, social, and psychological performance. Work experiences of the three groups are examined by placing each patient in a category of either regularly employed, sporadically employed, or unemployed; the quality of their performances on the job is assessed and reasons for job terminations noted.

Domestic performance is measured by a checklist on patients' household activities; each item is rated according to the degree to which the patient can perform the activity without assistance. The scale yields a domestic performance score that is totaled, averaged, and compared across groups. The scale was used by Angrist and Dinitz in other major works as well as by the researchers in the original ITC study.[11] It is described as reliable in the previous works but has weaknesses that are discussed with domestic performance results in the following chapters.

The social participation variable is measured by an activities scale that inquires into the behavior of the patient during the month preceding the follow-up interview and the usualness or unusualness of his behavior. Questions cover leisure time activities, friendship patterns, attendance at organizational meetings, and church attendance. This scale provides total participation scores that are averaged and compared across groups.

Treatment data secured from hospital and clinic records and a problems checklist are used in testing hypotheses one and two. One of the basic tools used throughout the ITC study, a behavior checklist is used as a valuable measure of the disturbance patients create in their homes.

SOs also answered a modified version of the Lorr IMPS scale, which gives an indication of patients' manifestation of disturbances in ideation, affect, motor activity, speech, and memory.[12] This scale, used routinely in the original home care study, proved to be consistent in measuring the degree of the patients' psychiatric distur-

11. Pasamanick, Scrapitti, and Dinitz, *Schizophrenics in the Community*, p. 96; Angrist et al., *Women After Treatment*, pp. 56–57.

12. Maurice Lorr, C. James Klett, Douglas M. McNair, and Julian Lasky, *Inpatient Multidimensional Psychiatric Scale* (IMPS) *Manual*.

bances.[13] It was demonstrated, during the original ITC study, that the psychiatrist's rating, nurse's ratings, and the SOs' ratings were sufficiently similar to permit substantial confidence in the SOs' description of the patients' psychiatric statuses.

Hypothesis Three

There has been no improvement in the patients' functioning on social, vocational, or domestic variables over their corresponding abilities during the original ITC home care experiment. (In short, we are assuming that over a long period of time the majority of schizophrenic patients deteriorate in their general patterns of adjustment.)

To test this hypothesis the patients' vocational, social, and domestic performances at follow-up in 1969 are compared with those at ITC intake in 1962.

A measure of social class, the Hollingshead two-factor index, gives us an assessment of patients' social-class mobility.[14] Interviews provide sufficient data on the patients' roles and familial behavior to allow us to evaluate their conformity, or lack of it, to social norms relating to age and sex behaviors in our society.

Our purpose therefore is to assess, first of all, the impact of the experimental program in terms of lasting effects on patient adjustments five years later at the time of the follow-up. Second, we are comparing the long-term adjustments of patients at follow-up with their statuses at intake to learn about patients' tendencies to either improve, remain status quo, or deteriorate in their adaptive patterns over time.

13. See Appendix B for all questionnaires and scales used in the follow-up.
14. August B. Hollingshead, "Two Factor Index of Social Position."

chapter two

Data Collection:
Procedures and Problems

The original ITC study results were available for comparison with follow-up findings. The major research forms from that study were also available for use, although some alterations were made in scales when questions had proven unsatisfactory or unproductive during the initial study, or when the longitudinal time factor, five years of elapsed time in the follow-up, demanded schedule revisions. Research forms were developed anew for the systematic collection of data from the clinic and hospital records and for the interviews with patients. Since each area of data collection required a different set of instruments and presented its own problems, each is considered separately in the following discussion.

Nurses as Interviewers: Unexpected Problems

Of the former ITC nurses, four were working for the state hospital in Louisville prior to the follow-up; they indicated a willingness to interview SOs and patients. It had been tacitly assumed that their prior knowledge of patients and relationships with them would be an advantage enjoyed by few follow-up research teams. But, in fact, their knowledge operated at times as an advantage and at other times as an unexpected disadvantage.

The nurses' interviews occurred either in the patients' homes or at the hospital; the majority took place in the homes. Visits were preceded by a letter sent to the patient's home that was signed by Dr. Davis, project director, who represented herself as a Kentucky Depatment of Mental Health consultant, with the approval of that department.[1]

During the original ITC study a number of patients were controls and others were study dropouts due to various reasons including their noncooperativeness. In the original study controls had been difficult people from whom to gain cooperation; questions and tests were time consuming and demanding, and in return ITC gave no services to them. It was difficult to justify repeated invasions of such patients' privacy; further, none of the staff had an incentive to develop good relationships with them. Nurses therefore anticipated rejections and difficulties with controls and dropouts and set aside these difficult cases until the end of the follow-up; that made the final period of data collection difficult and extremely slow. In reality not many of these difficult patients proved to be such when interviewed.

The period covered by the follow-up was lengthy, five years, and the information desired extensive; SO-interview forms encompassed 26 pages. The time required with the SO depended upon his mental and verbal capacities, the frequency of interruptions by household members, as well as upon the personality and skills of the nurse. Interviews lasted for one and a half to four hours; the average was two and a half hours. If the nurse wished also to complete a patient interview in the same home visit, another one half to full hour was needed.[2]

When the nurses first agreed to do these interviews it had been agreed to pay a set fee for each completed interview form; the amount was, then, felt to be fair by all concerned. It became apparent, later, that the fee was not adequate compensation. Lengthy forms and numerous call-backs to the homes had to be made to locate subjects, despite prior appointments; also available funds were being depleted by trips by the project director from her Ohio home to Kentucky. Funds were insufficient to compensate the nurses and researchers for all the work time put into the study. Without the nurses' devotion to the original ITC project and the strength of friendships formed during that study, it is unlikely that there would have been as much sacrificed to complete this project.

1. See Appendix A.
2. See Appendix B.

Eight months after work started it was apparent that the nurses could not complete the interviewing by fall of 1969, the preset deadline for terminating follow-up data collection. Therefore, two young women, both social-work students, were hired to finish the interviews with the difficult and noncooperative cases. The finished record of an unusually high case-location rate was due to the girls' youthful persistence.

Nurses were granted permission by the state hospital administration to interview patients attending the hospital's outpatient clinics near which they worked, or to visit patients who lived in areas of the city that they normally visited in the course of their work. Often patients lived in poor black neighborhoods or tough white areas, and because of riots and overt racial unrest in 1968–69 the women frequently found it necessary to go out in pairs and to avoid night calls. The follow-up work turned out to be more difficult, time consuming, and costly than anyone had initially expected; it was finally completed at the expense of donated time by the hospital and the nurses.

Location of the Study Population

Everything possible was done and every resource exhausted in locating a patient and his SO. Charts were drawn up on which every lead was noted and checked off when exhausted, until the clients were located or a "blank wall" was encountered.

The nurses' supervisor and the project director began patient location work with records that had been kept from the initial study. These files included each patient's ITC study address, the name of the SO, other relatives' names, phone numbers, and addresses. The outpatient clinic files of the state hospital were reviewed to confirm or update information on patients who had been recent clinic attenders. Extensive use was made, throughout, of telephone directories. When a patient or family member was located, the first letter was mailed and the case was assigned to the patient's original nurse.[3]

For patients not located by these preliminary efforts the search was continued in the following ways: other relatives were sent letters or called by phone requesting information about the patients' families; nurses, while out on calls, would stop at the patients' last

3. See Appendix A.

known addresses and ask neighbors about the family; past employers were consulted. All contacts were made as discreetly as possible. The state hospital's admissions card index was examined to locate the patient's latest address during his last readmission, if any, within the last five years. The general hospital's card index was also searched.

Many patients eluded these efforts, thus the next step was to send letters to the patient's last known address, via registered mail, with an address return request. Address return requests require post offices to trace patients and also ask the return of forms with results. Large city offices often did not take the time to consult their record books and simply returned the address requests with "address unknown" stamped upon them. Rural post offices were more likely to locate the people and to forward the letter. City and county directories were consulted extensively and on occasion all persons listed with the patients last names were called. The final effort made on patient location was a request to the city, county, and state public assistance agencies for help. A list of unlocated patients was sent to each agency director who was asked to indicate the name of any patient with whom the agency had a contact in the last five years. Also, in the year that it took to collect follow-up study data some patients were hospitalized and therefore they were located.

To find former patients took perseverance, ingenuity, and a lot of time. Relocation efforts proceeded remarkably well; only eight percent of the ITC population, or 18 cases out of the 226 original study people were completely lost. For the remaining 208 patients data were secured for all or part of the five research schedules.

Interviews with the Family

Usually when a patient was located the nurse and the project director exchanged ideas on the plan of approach to use; for some it was best to give no warning, in other cases a general contact letter was mailed.[4] Nurses arrived unannounced in cases where there may have been no phone or prior notification would have permitted the family to avoid the meeting or may have caused undue anxiety among family members.

In other cases it was necessary to make an appointment in order to find the SOs at home; especially if they were working husbands

4. See Appendix A.

or fathers. Appointments frequently were not kept, at times deliberately and sometimes by accident. This was not surprising for in this lower socioeconomic group appointment-keeping was not a part of the life style. Nurses had to persevere by returning again and again to homes and by making repeated appointments.

The nature of the nurses entrée depended upon the case. For some patients friendship aspects and renewed contact with the nurse were stressed, in others purely research interests were highlighted and the information was described as a valuable contribution to science; in all cases the research purpose was described and anonymity guaranteed.

Interviews with family members were usually held in the homes but others were held wherever possible; some took place on doorsteps, in drug stores, and, in one case, on a busy street corner. Since this follow-up did not deal with an original sample, each patient lost was irreplaceable and nurses were pressed to get the information at almost any cost. Results on data procurement testify to the effectiveness of the above philosophy.

Of the 152 SOs of hospital-referred patients, 85 percent were interviewed in person, less than 1 percent were interviewed over the phone, and in 8 percent of the cases the SO data were secured from records or other informants. In 6 percent of the cases there was absolutely no SO to be interviewed. Of all SOs, only 1 completely refused to be interviewed; many, it must be added, grudgingly permitted the interview.

The low refusal rate spoke for the tenacity of the interviewers as well as for the nature of the relationship nurses had formed with many of the patients and families. This does not mean that interview data were secured with ease. There were two major problems: first, the schedules were long and tiring to administer and, second, the nurses were not trained interviewers. Asking questions in a structured manner on seemingly irrelevant issues caused frustrations for them. This factor was noted during the original study when it was found that nurses were not at ease if they had to go into a home and simply talk to a patient; they were used to doing things and getting results. They were accustomed to public health nurses' tasks such as instructing a mother on how to bathe the new born baby or explaining the administration of insulin to a diabetic.

Nurses had felt compelled to offer direct advice when confronted with complaining families or delusional patients. It took time, experience, and supportive counsel to help the women see that their largest contribution was to listen, offer empathetic support, insist on the taking of medications, and in general act as a sounding board for the frequent, and hopefully cathartic, diatribes of patients and family.

The functions of a formal research interviewer differed drastically from such task-oriented doers, or even from empathetic and supportive listeners. Nurses had to learn to control an interview by limiting extraneous conversation, clarifying questions, probing into senstive areas, and continually maintaining rapport. The basic dilemma was to press for information while listening to problems families wanted to discuss. Although the nurses learned to handle the cumbersome SO interview form, they never liked it nor the formal purposes of the research interview.

The fact that nurses had, in most cases, long-term relationships with the families and had not seen most of them for years, made a formal interview format almost an affront to the interviewees. It was comparable to the situation that would occur if someone subjected a friend, after a long separation, to a formal interview. Once aware of the psychological ramifications, some nurses shrank from encounters with their favorite clients.

Reentering lives of people with whom the nurses had developed close relationships was problematic; nurses reacted variably to it. They were apprehensive of contacts with some patients because they feared learning the worst about their adjustments or disorder and trouble in their homes. They felt families would want or expect them to solve their problems as during the original ITC study. They also expressed guilt over renewing relationships with patients solely for the purpose of research; feeling that they should have shown an interest in the family during the past five years either for treatment or friendship purposes. Visits were often painful, traumatic, and sad; they were sometimes happy but seldom were they a simple job to be completed for the salary alone.

From the other side it was obvious that families were emotionally involved in seeing the nurse again. The majority were very pleased to hear from their ITC nurse and showed their pleasure but others expressed their feelings with anger and upset. One nurse barely escaped injury when a patient threw a sizeable rock at her windshield, shattering it, and saying, "Damn you . . . I don't want to see you again, get the H--- out of here."

Another family from which complete cooperation was expected greeted the nurse with, "Get out, I don't want to see ya and I ain't going to talk to ya." Weeks later, after repeated efforts, when the nurse gained entry she found that the patient had felt abandoned by her, and was angry for having been left at the end of the study. The patient explained it this way, "I used to wonder what I'd do if ya ever stopped comin' to see me and I used to worry about what'd happen to alla us and what I'd do. Then you didn't come. I went on . . . that's all."

A broad variety of responses were encountered. Some families, much to our chagrin and with some damage to our egos, indicated that they just could not remember ITC, or sometimes even their nurses. In some cases it was plausible for those who had received only brief ITC care, but in others the memory lapse was not as easy to explain except, perhaps, in pathological terms. Some families, especially those private cases in which the patients' function was very good, simply did not wish to remember a period of psychoses and were reluctant to be interviewed. Some were afraid that the nurses' visits foretold rehospitalization and they had to be reassured and reassured that this was not the case.

Many familiar circumstances had changed measurably and often the change, as we shall see, was for the worse. Such cases pressed the nurses to offer assistance and to return patients to psychiatric care facilities. The nurses were cautioned to avoid extensive entanglements, for their own benefit, but were not asked to avoid referral advice. In retrospect the interviews probably served as a valuable resource; many patients were sent to appropriate help sources. Conditions in some homes came as a shock to the nurses as well as to the project director who had known many of the families well. Some of the patients, for instance, had become the more stable member of the marital pair. One spouse was committed as a result of the nurse discovering her in a very active phase of a psychotic episode when the home was visited.

Nurses became depressed and dejected but also, sometimes, pleased with what they found. They reported feeling miscast as research interviewers and in making one trip visits to the patients' homes. The situation led us to believe that there was an inherent conflict between the humanitarian action-oriented role of the nurse and the rational noninvolved role of a researcher.

In some cases it was evident that a resumption of ITC-type case contacts with regular home visitation would have benefited and pleased all concerned whereas in other instances the women and families would be happy, if not relieved, to part company once again.

Patient Interviews

Patients were also interviewed but the format used to collect information from them differed measurably from the SO interview form.[5] The decision to include patient interviews was made on the basis of the past years of work with mental patients and the knowledge that patients formed relationships, talked about their problems, and, at times, related to others better than to family members. It seemed erroneous to assume that patients and families were totally different in their communicative abilities. A number of the patients had recovered and their spouses had become patients; in yet other cases the family members were at least as disturbed as the patient. Our goal was to give the patient a specific opportunity to express feelings about his illness, family, life situation, and treatment experience.

The quality and quantity of information expected from patient interviews rarely materialized. Patients exhibited responses that probably should have been expected of schizophrenics. They denied their illness or, when acknowledging it, spoke of it as a physical problem or regarded it simply as "nerves." Some projected past problems on family or events thereby consistently denying any personal responsibility for them. Most failed to see hospitalization or the original study's experimental contacts with ITC nurses as treatment. They felt that all they may have needed was rest or to be left alone. Some, the minority, acknowledged the helpfulness of medication and many noted the kindness or friendliness of the ITC nurses.

In contrast family members frequently praised the availability of ITC staff, during the original study, to talk with and the beneficial aspects of prescribed medications. One family member remarked, "This is the first time since the clinic (ITC) that anybody has talked to me about Cindy. They (the state outpatient clinic's personnel) just don't seem to want to know what she's doing at home."

Because patients tended to be more evasive, using denial frequent-

5. See Appendix B.

ly or responding in monosyllables or in single-word sentences, inter-viewing required skills different from those used with the SOs. The nurse had to gain the confidence of a respondent who was frequently suspicious, guarded, fearful of treatment persons, and who was, at times, floridly psychotic. Given the odds against gaining sufficiently good rapport to elicit true feelings, the nurses did well to get the information they secured. In retrospect it would probably have been better to have used structured rather than open-ended schedules for patient interviews.

Of the 152 original hospital-referred ITC patients 75 percent were interviewed. Less than 2 percent returned mailed questionnaires; 6.5 percent refused to be interviewed; 7 percent had died; and 10 per-cent were never located. The differential returns between patient interviews and those of SOs, 85 percent of the SOs interviewed versus 75 percent of the patients, suggests that SOs were more cooperative and that there were more of them from which to select interviewees; patients were a limited and set population. If an SO had died or could not be located a sister or another relative could be used as an alternative source, and when SOs could not be located data could sometimes be secured from hospital or clinic records.

If this follow-up's retrieval success is compared with previous re-search results it fared better than two studies and worse than one. The most outstanding job in sample location was accomplished by Myers and Bean.[6] Ten years after the initial study 355 (88 percent) of their available sample were interviewed. Nineteen percent of their original sample were private psychiatric care patients, and because of promises of confidentiality they were not available for restudy and had to be eliminated from the follow-up. It is doubtful that our re-trieval efforts were less rigorous than those by Myers and Bean; the differences may well be explained by the fact that the ITC patients were psychotics and, as a group, they are regarded as a highly dis-turbed population and therefore a less cooperative one. The retrieval rates of both studies attest to the feasibility of follow-up studies after long periods of elapsed time and demonstrate that losses can be held to tolerable levels.

In contrast the one-year follow-up by Simmons and Freeman showed a loss of 9 percent of the sample within one month after the start of the program and an additional 6 percent loss in the next eleven months; a total of 15 percent of the sample lost by the end of

6. Myers and Bean, *A Decade Later*, p. 22.

the first year.[7] Less successful were the efforts of Michaux and associates. Out of 218 study members they lost 79 for a 36.2 percent loss in the first month. In 22 percent of the cases data was substantially missing by the end of the one-year study. This added up to a total loss rate of 58.2 percent—a substantial portion of the sample. They explain their losses in the following manner, "A candidate might understandably react adversively when having freshly left the hospital and returned home he was contacted by a person not previously known to him and asked to report his condition."[8]

We dwell on the above not simply to draw attention to the relocation rate in this study but to highlight those elements that contributed to effective retrieval: (1) research access to agency records and agency cooperativeness (an essential); (2) letters signed by known treatment persons or by the mental hygiene department for introductory purposes; (3) home visitations giving only minimal forewarning; (4) utilization of family members to secure cooperation from patients; (5) interviews in the home (this includes psychiatrist who may be needed to evaluate patients); (6) uniformed staff recognizable as agents of the mental hygiene department (uniforms demonstrating affiliations with authority are of value with lower-class persons only); (7) prior personal knowledge by the interviewers about the family and patients whenever possible; and (8) persistence!

Going out to homes, meeting family and patients on their grounds and presenting oneself at the door makes it difficult for the family to refuse a friendly nurse or social worker. Families usually invite someone inside who acts as though he expects to come in. After gaining entrance the family must be extremely rude to exclude a researcher who desires to remain. Determination and a friendly attitude are necessary ingredients in a follow-up. For instance, one of the patients refused to allow the nurse in the home so the interview took place through a locked screen door. Yet another patient and her husband were so evasive that the social worker, after tracking them down to his newspaper stand, conducted the interview on the street corner of a busy downtown thoroughfare. Though often conducted under less than ideal conditions, the contacts and interviews provided us with a thorough picture of patient adjustment in the community.

7.   Freeman and Simmons, *The Mental Patient Comes Home*, pp. 29–30.
8.   Michaux et al., *The First Year Out*, pp. 23–25.

Hospital and Clinic Records

The remaining area of data collection dealt with the systematic review of hospital and clinical records.[9] Negative comments found in the sociological literature about the use of agency records in research were confirmed by our experiences. Hospitals did not keep records for our convenience; their bulk and what seemed to be near random order posed frustrations to systematic research. Each new hospital administration presented the likelihood that a new filing method would be initiated and the record format changed.

The consistency of a patient's illness, over time, was of interest in the follow-up, hence the final diagnosis that appeared in the hospital discharge summary was needed. In reality doctors, at times, forgot to include the diagnosis and sometimes the entire summary. Another area of special concern was family interaction, the most useful document for such information was the social history taken by social workers shortly after the patient's admission. However, approximately four years prior to the follow-up the state hospital administrations ceased to require histories; they were considered too time consuming to acquire. Once a social history was eliminated there was little in the medical records about patients' social adjustments or family. Records contained clinical information about the patient's general emotional state, his affect, memory, physical ills, abilities to perform hospital chores, and the medications administered.

Occasionally an occupational and vocational therapy note appeared reading something like this, "The patient attends OT (occupational therapy) daily. He seems to like it." Or, "John works in the kitchen, he doesn't complain and goes willingly every day." The majority of the notes contained nurses' commentary on the cleanliness, appearance, and general cooperativeness of the patient. Notes appeared in profusion when the patient became a management problem, that is, highly aggressive or disruptive of the lives of other patients or of the staff. Almost all patients were disruptive at some time or another during their stay.

The most glaring inadequacies of the mental hospital are the lack of individualized information about personality dynamics or of interpersonal relationships among patients. There were some exceptions: the old social histories, the case histories written by medical students at the general hospital who did this as part of their educa-

9. See Appendix C.

tional assignments, an occasional note by a nurse or aide who had formed a relationship with the patient and took the time to report a conversation, or the occasional report of a doctor or social worker who had become personally concerned about a patient. The lack of personalization appeared to be a system fault due to the persistence of hospital medical traditions of rational medical authority, and the excessively high ratio of patients to clinical personnel; a defect resulting from the historic chronic under-funding and under-staffing of state mental facilities.

It was also evident that people rarely read a patient's history aside from the diagnosis. Looking systematically through a chart the researcher was confronted with repeated errors and misjudgments made about patients that could probably have been averted if the personnel had read about the patient's social situation and his history. Hollingshead and Duff suggest that a similar situation prevails in the general medical hospital.[10]

Glaringly absent from the charts were notes concerning interaction between the hospital treatment staff and the family. When, on occasion, the staff saw families on the wards they recorded a simple note such as, "John's mother visited him today. He was agitated for some time after she left." Otherwise the hospital staff did not interact with a family member, and when the patient was ready to go home the family was simply notified to come and pick him up. Upon release the patient may or may not have received a referral to a follow-up clinic, and frequently he would not follow this directive to attend, if he received it.

Securing data from the clinics was as difficult as the collection of information from the private psychiatric hospitals primarily because there were so many facilities involved. Emphasis since the early 1960s had been upon community care in mental health. Many community clinics had been started in the late 1960s and a substantial number of the hospital's expatients had been referred to them. Hospital administrators encouraged referrals to after-care clinics because they could not afford to staff their own clinics. They insisted that the community clinics, amply funded, carry the burden. Patients frequently were caught in a rotating referral system, a system of buck-passing between hospital and clinics. The end result of this was added confusion for the patient and his subsequent withdrawal from

10. August B. Hollingshead and Raymond S. Duff, *Sickness and Society.*

care, a situation easily precipitated under the best of circumstances. It would perhaps be more professional to call this situation organizational confusion resulting from too rapid social change.

Each clinic's director was called personally by the project director and asked to check his files for ITC project patients. Release of information forms signed by the patients were supplied per the administrators' requests.[11] In some cases the researchers filled out the clinic research forms and in others the clinic directors and social workers volunteered their time to do them. Even when cooperation was exceedingly good the collection process was slow due to the number of clinics involved. Some of the patients had been treated in as many as five different clinics. All together twelve clinics were involved as well as four private hospitals, three federal hospitals, and six state hospitals.

Clinic records were generally highly informative because the personnel working in clinics were more interactionally and analytically oriented than the staff in the hospitals. Conversely, even the best clinics were not as proficient in the administration and charting of prescriptions as were hospitals.

The data from private and other state hospitals were secured via mail as hospital superintendents were asked to answer specific questions about a patient's treatment experiences. The requests for information were sent out with the cooperation of the Central State Hospital superintendent.

Description of the Sample

In that this study is a follow-up, the population and its characteristics are predetermined by the original ITC study. The ambulatory home care (GP-referred) patients from the original study are not included in the follow-up evaluation that follows because they represent a separate group due to their private referral source. Inclusion of that data would unnecessarily expand this document without adding qualitatively to the report.

All but 5 percent of the home care drug patients, 9 percent of the home care placebo patients, and 11 percent of the controls were located. The controls understandably showed the highest loss rate for they were the least personally well known by the researchers. De-

---

11. See Appendix C.

spite this differential loss rate by categories, the data showed that there were no statistically significant differences between the study groups on the demographic characteristics.

Demographic Variables

At ITC intake (1962) the groups did not differ on age, sex, or race; the only manner in which they might have changed after five years would have been for the researchers to have lost, by death or non-location, disproportionate numbers of cases in the three groups. This did not happen (see table 1). Therefore we rest assured that we continue to deal with a randomly distributed population.

TABLE 1

DEMOGRAPHIC CHARACTERISTICS OF STUDY
GROUPS AT FOLLOW-UP (1969)
(In Percent)

Characteristic	Drug Group N=57	Placebo Group N=41	Control Group N=48
Male	38.3	30.1	30.6
Black.	31.9	33.4	35.2
Mean age[a].	42.1	43.0	43.4
High school graduate . . .	35.9	32.8	16.5
Not married.	62.0	59.0	62.9
No residential moves (in last five years) . .	37.9	52.8	42.0
Patient is economically independent[b]	61.8	68.5	60.1
Welfare recipient.	38.3	61.2	41.3
Socioeconomic status mean scores.	58.7	60.5	63.7

[a]In years.

[b]Patients were considered economically independent if they were not reliant upon relatives (other than spouse) for income, therefore some patients who were welfare recipients were categorized as economically independent.

Of the home care drug group 38 percent were males, of the home care placebo and of the control group 30 percent were males. The percentage of patients who were white was 68 percent, 66 percent, and 65 percent for the drug, placebo, and control groups respectively. On mean age the three groups were within one year of each other (patients were 43 years old on the average). Women outnumbered the men by almost two to one, a fact reflecting the higher ratio of female to male schizophrenics admitted to the original ITC program because of the relatively greater willingness of relatives to accept their female patients at home.[12] Racially, the study population under represented the percentage of white schizophrenics at Central Hospital, which was 79 percent; the ITC sample had some 10 percent fewer whites and 10 percent more blacks than were to be found at Central.[13] Black families were somewhat more inclined to provide for and take home their sick relatives.

Regarding other demographic characteristics, during the initial ITC study it was found that: "The . . . 152 patients in the three study groups, home on drugs (57), home on placebos (41), and hospital controls (54), were similar to each other in almost all the important demographic characteristics except that the controls were significantly lower in education and higher in residential mobility."[14] The three study groups, at the follow-up (1969), no longer showed any significant differences on any variables including education and residential mobility (see table 1).

More patients were single than married, continued confirmation of the inability of many of the mentally ill to marry and to stay married. The majority of the patients had some independent sources of support and did not have to depend on parents or husbands. The patients' socioeconomic status remained quite low. The mean score for the drug group was 59; 61 for the placebo group, and 64 for the controls.[15] The worst possible score on the Hollingshead Index was 77 and the patients averaged 62, placing them in social classes IV and V.

The patients low economic status was further attested to by their employment status. Approximately 40 percent of those who were neither housewives or students received or existed on some form of public assistance or insurance; either federal-state Aid to the Permanently and Totally Disabled, federal Social Security payments to the

12. Pasamanick, Scarpitti, and Dinitz, *Schizophrenics in the Community*, p. 82.
13. Ibid., p. 81.
14. Ibid., pp. 81–82.
15. Measures of socioeconomic status depended upon the August B. Hollingshead, "Two Factor Index of Social Position."

disabled, or monies received through Aid for Dependent Children. Thirty-eight percent of the drug group were welfare recipients, as were 61 percent of the placebo patients, and 41 percent of the controls. Clearly the patients, overall, were impaired in the area of employment and vocational self-support.[16] Educationally the vast majority of the patients had not completed high school, including 64 percent of the drug group, 67 percent of the placebo group, and 83 percent of the controls. Such factors assisted in explaining their low economic position.

During ITC 54 percent of the drug group, 44 percent of the placebo group, and 52 percent of the controls were married. In each study group at follow-up there were approximately 10 percent fewer marrieds, a rather substantial drop in marital stability since ITC. During ITC 25 percent of the drug group, 27 percent of the placebo group, and 17 percent of the controls had never married. In the intervening years the numbers had dropped to 19, 20, and 11 percent, respectively, in each group. In short, it was evident that many patients in each group had since married and divorced and that there was substantial marital turmoil and disruption. In Chapter 4 marital statuses will be examined further but these facts are given here as a sample of the difficulties and instabilities that patients experienced in maintaining close interpersonal relations.

To summarize the main points, these patients were lower-class people who, if not dependent upon family members economically, were dependent upon welfare. They included disproportionate numbers of women and blacks as compared to the average population. In essence the groups overall were comprised of marginal role members in our society.

Over the follow-up period there was no positive tendency by patients to improve their social situation, they had not significantly increased their educational level nor their socioeconomic status. These facts combined with the figures on marital instabilities begin to indicate that patients at best remained in status quo or had slipped backward in their social adjustments. Also, demographic data showed that we had adequately located the original sample and assured the validity of cross-group comparisons at follow-up, the task we undertake in our next chapter.

16. Reasons for the disproportionate welfare support among placebo patients are given in Chapter 4.

chapter three

Patients' Psychiatric Status and Treatment Experiences

In this chapter we shall present the findings in regard to the patients' psychiatric adjustments at follow-up in 1969. The analysis presented first compares the original study groups to adjudge if the home care drug patients were able to maintain the better adjustment advantage they held when ITC ended. Aside from information on the impact or lasting effects of differential forms of treatment on the mental states of schizophrenics this analysis provides some general insights into patients' long-range patterns of adaption. The second analysis presented focuses upon the deterioration or improvement of each patient judged against his mental status in 1962 at ITC intake as compared with his status through and up to follow-up in 1969.

There has been debate in the psychiatric literature about whether rehospitalization is the best, or even a good, measure of a patient's mental status. Our experience with ITC data confirms that patients with the worst psychiatric evaluations are, in fact, the most likely to be rehospitalized. During the follow-up all patients' psychiatric statuses were evaluated by the SO. The form used was the revised Inpatient Multidimensional Psychiatric Scale, hereafter called the Lorr IMPS; this same instrument was also used in the original ITC study.

During the original ITC study the Lorr IMPS scale was used by the psychiatrist, the nurse, and the SO simultaneously. When these three reports were compared the ITC researchers found that the evaluations of patients were very similar except that nurses generally noted less pathology (as reflected in lower total scale scores) than the psychiatrist; SOs, in turn, saw even less pathology. Since SO evaluations corresponded closely to the mental status ratings of psychiatrists and nurses, these reports were considered to be a reliable measure, if in fact a conservative one, of the patients' mental conditions during the follow-up.[1]

Study Groups Compared at Follow-up (1969)

Table 2 contains the mental status scores of the drug, placebo, and hospital control patients at the time of the follow-up in 1969.[2] To

TABLE 2

PSYCHIATRIC SCALE MEAN SCORES FOR STUDY GROUPS
AT FOLLOW-UP (1969)

Scale Factor	Maximum Possible Score	Drug Group N=57	Placebo Group N=41	Control Group N=45
A Excitement.	9	1.58	1.79	2.02
C Paranoid ideation	49	5.74	7.00	8.27
G Bizarre motor behavior.	14	2.20	2.29	2.89
H Hostile agitation	8	.62	1.80	2.29
E Feelings of depression.	18	1.82	1.53	2.49
F Perceptual distortions.	19	.40	1.24	.66
I Retardations and apathy	9	1.69[a]	1.16	2.22[a]
J Grandiose ideation.	27	1.91	.26	.63
K Thinking disorganization and bizarre speech.	7	1.03	.50	.72
D Disorientation.	6	.03	.09	.04
Total weighted score	166	17.02	17.67	22.22
Excitement-retardation	8	1.57	2.43	2.09
Perceptual and thinking distortions	74	6.81	9.02	9.56
Schizophrenia score.	36	4.90	4.21	5.73

[a]The difference between the drug and control group reached the .05 level of statistical significance.

1. Pasamanick, Scarpitti, and Dinitz, *Schizophrenics in the Community*, pp. 91–94.
2. Later in this chapter we shall compare the follow-up status of patients to their status at ITC intake and at the termination of ITC care.

assist in understanding the Lorr scale we offer the following description. The Lorr scale has 75 items answerable by yes or no; differential weights assigned to each item range from zero to eight. A no answer is scored as zero. The higher the weight the sicker the behavior and the more that factor's score counts toward a high total score. Factors such as "excitability" are determined by combinations of items. For instance, Factor A contains nine separate behavior items dispersed at random throughout the scale, each with a possible value of one; therefore the maximal score for Factor A is nine. Table 2 shows the maximal possible scores for each factor. Hypothetically a very ill person could have a maximum score of 166 and an entirely well person could score zero. The subscale scores, such as excitement-retardation, consist of varieties of combinations of the individual factors.

Of concern in the analysis of mental status is the question: Did the groups differ appreciably from one another at the time of the follow-up in 1969? It will be recalled that the home care drug patients had an advantage (a better average score) during the initial study. Table 2 shows that the mean scores of the three treatment groups at follow-up do not differ significantly on any of the psychiatric inventory factors, with one exception; the control group is significantly different from the placebo group on Factor I, retardation apathy. On the subscales, the schizophrenia index scores were 4.90, 4.21, and 5.73 for the drug, placebo, and control groups respectively. The other two morbidity scores, excitement-retardation and thinking distortion, followed a similar pattern showing no major differences among the study groups. We concluded therefore that five years after the ITC experiment the groups were no longer different in psychiatric status, that is, the home care drug group, which had shown a superior status during the experiment in 1962, was unable to maintain its advantage once home care was withdrawn and as the follow-up years passed.

By the time of the follow-up, all of the groups had relatively sizeable scores, proportionate to their totals, on Factor A, excitement, Factor C, paranoid ideation, and Factor H, hostile agitation. All study groups yielded substantial scores on Factor G, bizarre behavior, which meant that they were reported to be walking, standing, sitting, moving about, grinning, giggling, or making faces in strange ways, as well as talking to themselves when no one else was around. Such behavioral manifestations may be adjudged to be overt evidence of paranoid thought processes. Paranoid ideation consists of beliefs about being persecuted, cheated, plotted against, talked about, and controlled by others. Symptom patterns vary within cultures, among cultures, as well as within any one society over time. In the United States today, paranoid symptomatology and diagnoses are widespread especially among hospitalized patients.[3] Our patient population not only continued to manifest psychiatric symptoms five years after ITC intake, but did so in a manner reflective of the American culture in general.

Longitudinal Comparisons (1964–1969)

The longitudinal evaluations that follow involve a comparison of the patients' mental status at ITC intake in 1962 with the final ITC evaluation in 1964 and the follow-up study findings, conducted five years later, in 1969. This analysis provides dramatic evidence about the differential effect of various types of treatment programs on schizophrenics' mental statuses. Looking at table 3 it is possible to view the impact of the ITC home care program on the drug and placebo groups. At intake the drug group's total mean score was 28.0 and by ITC's termination it dropped to 10.2, indicating the impact of drugs plus ITC socio-environmental supportive care;[4] the placebo group's mean score at intake was 38.5 and by the termination of ITC it had dropped to 20.6. ITC had a salutary impact upon both groups but left the placebo patients with the higher score, the "sicker" of the two groups; this result was attributed to the lack of drug care during ITC for placebo patients. Similarly over the course of ITC care, improvements in scores were noted on the other two indices. On the schizophrenic-disorganization score the impact of ITC care was similar; again the placebo patients did show some benefits from home care even though they remained the sicker group at the end of ITC, as evidenced by their higher scores.

By the time of the follow-up (1969), as shown in table 3, the reported mean score for the drug group was *higher* than at the ITC

3. For a discussion of the effects of variant cultures upon schizophrenic symptoms and diagnoses see H. B. M. Murphy, E. D. Wittkower, J. Fried, and H. Ellenberger, "A Cross-Cultural Survey of Schizophrenic Symptomatology," pp. 237–49.

4. Socio-environmental support as herein used refers to home visitations by treatment personnel inclusive of counseling with families and patients plus the provision of social services to the entire family in the area of vocational, recreational, and medical care referrals to appropriate agencies.

TABLE 3

PSYCHIATRIC SCALE MEAN SCORES COMPARED AT ITC INTAKE (1962),
ITC TERMINATION (1964), AND FOLLOW-UP (1969)

	DRUG GROUP			PLACEBO GROUP		
	ITC Intake N=55	ITC End N=49	Follow-Up N=57	ITC Intake N=41	ITC End N=31	Follow-Up N=41
Total weighted scores. .	28.0	10.2	17.0	38.5	20.6	17.7
Perceptual and thinking distortion. .	12.1	2.8	6.8	19.5	7.9	9.0
Schizophrenic disorganization. . . .	7.8	4.0	4.9	10.3	8.1	4.2

project termination. It had increased from 10.2 at the end of ITC (1964) to 17.0 at the time of the follow-up (1969). This signals the decrease in the favorable psychiatric adaptation of such patients once the socio-environmental treatment given by ITC was withdrawn. In direct contrast, the placebo group's mean mental status score was *lower* at the follow-up than at the end of ITC. The placebo group dropped from 20.6 at the end of ITC to 17.7 at the follow-up. This is dramatic evidence of the fact that, although socio-environmental support alone had an impact on psychiatric placebo patients during the original ITC study, the initiation of drug therapy by outpatient clinics after the termination of ITC acted to further improve these patients' mental statuses. These findings also tell us that the home care drug patients received maximal benefits from the medications and socially supportive attention given during the original study and that they worsened when ITC come care was withdrawn, a period in which they received only routine outpatient care. Conversly, the placebo group of patients, deprived of drugs during the project, improved after leaving ITC when, in the course of their routine outpatient treatment, they received drugs.

By the time of the follow-up, as noted in the previous section, the placebo group's mean score was indistinguishable from that of the drug group; 17.7 for the placebo patients and 17.0 for the drug group. The lowering of adjustments among the drug group and the improvement among the placebo patients, post ITC, tended to equalize the groups by the time of the follow-up in 1969. By that time there were no significant differences in the mental status reports among the study groups. These findings support hypothesis one, that no differences would be found. General conclusions can thus be drawn about the most advantageous form of treatment, which is drug attention *plus* socio-environmental support; this is followed by drug attention alone, and as least desireable socio-environmental support alone. In short, ITC care, when it consisted of drugs plus socio-environmental support, was the superior treatment to any other form of care. It should be noted that patients were referred to state and municipal outpatient clinics or to the mental hospital facilities when ITC terminated. In these facilities the care given usually consists of drugs and counseling (at times) to the patient only, excluding most families, and excluding a focus upon the family group as a microcosm within which the patient's disorder is an interactive phenomenon.

Hospitalization Experiences during ITC
and the Follow-up Period

Since all patients were either hospitalized and/or treated at the Institute Treatment Center we know that all patients experienced some form of treatment between 1961 and the termination of the ITC home care project in 1964. We also know that during the original study ITC saved the home care drug patients, as compared to the controls, a significant number of in-hospital days. The home care drug patients spent 10 percent of the study time in the hospital, the home care placebo patients 20 percent, and the controls 25 percent (see figure 1). Part of this differential was due to the initial hospitalization treatment of the controls (which averaged 83 days), part to the early removal of home care drug patients from hospitals, and part to the successful impact of the ITC socio-supportive and drug treatment program on the home care drug group.

Therefore, looking at the hospitalization histories over the follow-up's five-year period the question to be answered is: Did the ITC care program have any long term or lasting impact, or had the groups by the time of the follow-up become comparable on their hospitalization histories? As displayed in table 4, the data show that the drug, placebo, and hospital control patients averaged over 1,604 days each at home (at risk) after the termination of the ITC program. During this time, 39 percent of the drug, 39 percent of the control, and 43 percent of the placebo patients (see figure 2) had remained continuously at home. This means that 61 percent of the drug and control patients required hospitalization as well as 57 percent of the placebo patients; none of these differences in hospital care experiences following ITC were statistically significant.

The drug, placebo, and hospital controls each averaged 125, 221, and 136 days of hospitalization, respectively, as presented in table 4, between ITC termination and the follow-up in 1969. These differences, despite their comparative magnitudes, were not statistically significant. In percentage terms (see table 4) the hospitalized in the drug, placebo, and control groups spent 11, 18, and 16 percent, respectively of the follow-up time period in inpatient hospital care.

None of the findings on the hospital experiences showed a significant difference among the groups with one meaningful exception; the home care drug patients, when compared to the placebo group, spent a significantly longer time *at home* before their first hospitalization

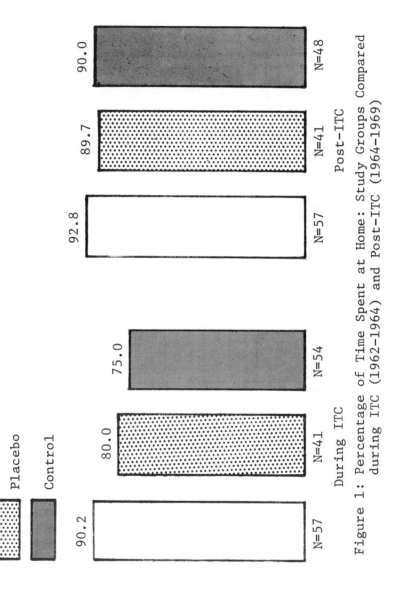

Figure 1: Percentage of Time Spent at Home: Study Groups Compared during ITC (1962–1964) and Post-ITC (1964–1969)

TABLE 4

DURATION OF HOSPITALIZATIONS COMPARED AMONG STUDY GROUPS
OVER THE FOLLOW-UP (1964 TO 1969)

Duration of Hospitalization	Drug Group N=57	Placebo Group N=41	Control Group N=48
Mean days at home over the follow-up.	1,692	1,604	1,690
Mean days in the hospital.	125	221	136
Mean days at home before first hospitalization (after ITC termination)	354[a]	166[a]	417
Mean days of first hospitalization.	130	256	126
Percentage of follow-up time in the hospital (of those hospitalized).	11.2	18.0	16.1
Percentage of follow-up time in the hospital (of the entire group).	7.2	10.3	10.0

[a]Differences between the drug and placebo groups were significant at the .05 level of confidence.

(see table 4). The drug group averaged 354 days at home (once the ITC home care ended) before hospitalization, versus 166 days for the placebo patients; the difference was significant at the .05 level of confidence. This finding shows that home care only had a lasting effect for approximately a single year after the program ended.

Table 4 shows that placebo patients entered the hospital sooner once the support of ITC home care was withdrawn; many of the stalwarts who had survived home care without drugs failed soon after ITC, having neither the drugs nor the staff's attentions to support them. The placebo group spent nearly 85 more days, on the average, in the hospital during the following-up than the controls and 96 days more than the drug patients, which suggested that they needed more extensive chemotherapeutic attention than the others. The placebo group made up for the absence of drug attention during ITC home care by longer time periods spent under psychiatric care after ITC ended. This finding once again emphasizes the necessity for drugs as an integral part of psychiatric care for schizophrenics.

Looking at figure 2 it is obvious that the rehospitalization expe-

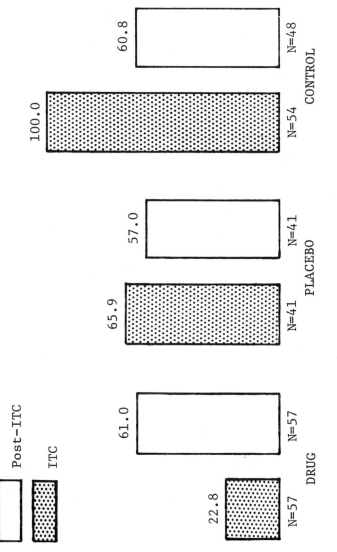

Figure 2: Percentage of Each Study Group Hospitalized: ITC (1962–1964) Compared with Post-ITC (1964–1969)

riences of the study groups in the follow-up period, 1964–69 (post-ITC home care) were very similar (the percentage of patients hospitalized over the follow-up study period equalized with the passage of time). Whereas some 77 percent of the home care drug group avoided hospitalization during ITC, only 39 percent managed to avoid it during the follow-up. This again points to the salutary effect of socio-environmental home care support when drugs are provided. In contrast (see figure 2), all controls experienced hospitalizations during the initial study but 39 percent stayed out during the follow-up. Since ITC's end then, the groups had equalized their hospitalization experiences and the differential impact of ITC care was no longer visible by the follow-up in 1969. Once ITC home care was *withdrawn*, patients who were given similar post-ITC treatment experiences became alike on psychiatric and hospitalization experiences. The prior data offers clear testimony to the differential impact of varying treatment programs and to the fact that care must be an ongoing enterprise for this group of psychiatric patients if our goal is to reduce the incidence of hospitalization.[5]

Outpatient Clinic History: Follow-up (1964-1969)

We can not draw conclusions about patient functioning based only on psychiatric hospitalization experiences, even though we will document the fact that the most disturbed patients are, on the average, hospitalized more frequently. Occasionally quite disturbed patients remain outside of the hospital and function adequately; also some comparatively healthy patients are hospitalized for reasons that may be unrelated to psychopathology. To gain a more complete view of the care received by the study groups, the outpatient clinic treatment experiences over the five years between 1964 and 1969 are reviewed.

Clinic attenders can not, prima facie, be considered sick, certainly not in the same way that hospitalized patients are defined as ill or in need of care. Outpatient hospital clinics are usually considered resources for the provision of assistance to patients to prevent the recurrence of psychiatric problems, that is, they are used as post-hospital maintainance resources. In reality the uses of these clinics are quite variable. Patients attend because they are disturbed and they, or their families, hope that rehospitalization can be avoided;

5. See table 18 in the Appendix D, for lifetime hospitalization comparisons.

others attend because they feel well and consider the clinic a means for continuing this well-being; others, also long time exhospitalized patients, attend purely for social contacts otherwise lacking, for them, in the community.

The philosophy regarding outpatient care encompasses many treatment orientations including acute crisis intervention, the regulation of drug maintenance, psychiatric and social rehabilitation, and, also, preventive attention for patients never hospitalized. It was not, therefore, as easy to interpret data on clinic care as clear evidence of a patient's illness. These data nonetheless provide some valuable insights.

In table 5 it is apparent that the clinic data complement the hos-

TABLE 5

CLINIC TREATMENT EXPERIENCES OF STUDY GROUPS
DURING THE FOLLOW-UP (1964 - 1969)

Clinic Care	Drug Group N=49	Placebo Group N=40	Control Group N=37
Mean number of clinic contacts (1964--a five-month period).	2.0	2.1	1.4
Mean contacts (1965)	3.2	3.3	2.7
Mean contacts (1966)	3.0	3.4	3.2
Mean contacts (1967)	3.4	3.0	2.2
Mean contacts (1968)	2.1	3.0	2.3
Mean contacts (1969--a five- month period).	1.4	2.1	1.8
Total contacts over the follow- up (1964-1969)	15.2	16.9	13.5
Mean number of days under out- patient care over the follow- up (1964-1969)	647	807	623
Percentage of time, when not hospitalized, in clinic care (1964-1969)	37.0	47.3	35.1

pitalization data previously reported in this chapter. The first variable, on the mean number of patient contacts, shows that both the placebo patients and the home care drug patients followed through and attended the clinics per the referrals given them by the social worker when ITC home care terminated in 1964. Through the years of 1965 and 1966 the placebo patients attended the clinic more frequently (making 3.3 trips per year) than the drug and control group patients, who averaged slightly fewer visits (between 2.7 and 3.2 per year). Statistically the differences are not significant. From table 4 we learned that the placebo patients were most often hospitalized over the follow-up; also they had been hospitalized significantly sooner than the drug patients in the post-ITC period. They were, therefore, not as available for outpatient care during the early follow-up period, a fact that also explained their return to clinic care later in the follow-up. From table 5, we note that in 1968 the placebo patients averaged 3.0 visits compared to the 2.1 and 2.3 average numbers for the drug and control patients. Placebo patients appeared to have needed more clinic attention; their total clinic contacts between 1964 and 1969 were 16.9, the drug group's contacts were 15.2, and the control's 13.5. The placebo group patients averaged more total days under care, 807, versus 647 for the drug group, and 623 for the controls. The percentage of eligible home time, that is, the time at home when the patients were not hospitalized, underscored the previous findings: the placebo patients were under clinic care 47 percent of their time at home, the drug group 37 percent of the time, and the controls 35 percent of the time. Thus, the placebo group's patients were recipients of more outpatient care as well as more care in the hospital during the follow-up; again this was due to drug deprivation during the ITC experimental care study. These data clarify the fact that clinics, like hospitals, are used by patients as treatment resources or as crisis centers, not as rehabilitation facilities; patients appear to use clinics when they are actively emotionally disturbed. Further analyses of clinic useage are presented in Chapter 5.

Conclusions

Five years later, the statistics made it abundantly clear that whatever ITC home care did in the early 1960s, its positive impact had lasted, at best, for six months to one year after the original project's termination. Five years later no statistically significant difference between the groups was found to exist on either psychological-functioning, hospital-treatment, or clinic care received; the impact of ITC's care had been wholly eroded. Hypothesis one, which postulated this fact, was therefore supported. Rather than viewing this as evidence of the failure of the ITC experiment we see it as clear evidence for the need to continue active treatment of schizophrenics and to avoid viewing such patients as either rehabilitated or cured.

Data analysis on the level of patients' functioning also lends support to hypothesis three, which states that the groups would not demonstrate measurable improvement over time in their adjustments. The placebo group proved the exception to this hypothesis; they showed improvement in their psychiatric status once ITC terminated because of subsequent drug care, therefore we could not accept the third hypothesis without this qualification. Regardless of the circumstances surrounding the placebo patients, a result we had forgotten to consider when formulating the hypotheses, all groups continued to exhibit a recurrent need for care and psychiatric attention, thereby demonstrating the chronic and episodic nature of the schizophrenic disorder. Further evidence of the disabling nature of the illness is presented in the next chapter when the five-year community functioning of the study groups is analyzed in terms of their social, domestic, and vocational performance variables.

The data also suggest the following types of interaction between the illness and varying treatment approaches. The disorder is episodic, chronic, and tends to persist at a level of severity usually suggested early in its course. The latter information is further supported by the analysis in Chapter 5. Chemotherapy is necessary and the use of drugs is the best insurance against recurrent debilitating episodes; this was the major finding of the original ITC study and it is supported by the follow-up data. As social, economic, and familial supports are added to drug care the patients show their optimal adjustment. This conclusion is supported by Philip R. May, who did an extensive study of the results of treatment, of differing types, on the adjustment outcomes of schizophrenics. He found that, "Drugs alone, and psychotherapy plus drugs, were the most effective treatments and also the least costly in time and money."[6] He also found that milieu therapy and psychotherapy, used alone, were not effective, nor were the majority of the electroshock treatments given in the state hospitals. This is analogous to this study's findings on the superiority of drug therapy when combined with social home care.

6.   Philip R. May, *Treatment of Schizophrenia*.

chapter four

Patients' Community Adjustments

In the previous chapter the experiences of the drug, placebo, and control groups were examined using measures of patients' mental status: in-hospital treatment and outpatient clinic care. Findings using such variables are valuable in and of themselves but, as most students of emotional disorders know, hospitalization and official treatment experiences provide only a partial picture of patients' adjustments and of their mental health. Disordered patients have been known to avoid formal treatment agents and relatively well patients have sought and secured treatment. For instance, Freeman and Simmons, Pasamanick, Dinitz, Angrist, and most recently Molholm, report that patient performance on domestic functioning does not necessarily provide an indication of a patient's treatment or psychiatric status.[1]

The original ITC home care study demonstrated that some psychotic patients held responsible jobs, for example, a nurse in a surgery room, a school teacher, and an assembly-line operator of heavy machinery, and that these patients performed their jobs well. However, the majority of our patients were incapacitated and unable to work outside of their homes or, sometimes, inside their homes.

During ITC home care most patients were grossly deficient social-

1. Freeman and Simmons, *The Mental Patient Comes Home*; Pasamanick, Scarpitti, and Dinitz, *Schizophrenics in the Community*; Angrist et al., *Women After Treatment*; Molholm, "Female Mental Patients and Normal Female Controls."

ly in activities requiring interpersonal competence but, as with vocational and domestic performance, such inadequacies did not inevitably lead to psychiatric care. Conversely, some ITC patients were quite socially adequate; for example, one woman raised twelve children, socialized, played bingo almost nightly, and also had a full-time job. Relationships between social, interpersonal, domestic, and vocational competence and psychiatric disorders were not, therefore, highly predictive of needs for formal care and are therefore not well understood in terms of their importance in precipitating or predicting overt mental problems.

This chapter will present an examination of the patients' social, domestic, and vocational adjustments over the follow-up and will work toward an understanding of how mentally disordered behavior is expressed socially and in specific task areas. The study groups, drug, placebo, and control, are compared with each other, and their follow-up status is also compared with their performance levels at the beginning, and at the end, of ITC home care. The reader is also advised of our findings on the problems in long-term community adjustments of the patients.

Patients as Problems

As our study of ITC patients took place (over a total of eight years) it became clear to us that the average schizophrenic behaved in a problematic fashion. Families worry about patients, are upset by them, and frequently commit them to state and private treatment agencies. State personnel also show apprehension as evidenced by their policy of confining patients in facilities that preclude patients' interaction with the community. In many ways patients upset and frighten people.

Thomas Szasz says that patients violate minor social norms, not mores and not laws but the unspoken proprieties of social behavior, such proprieties that we usually take for granted. Szasz also defines mental illness as a "problem in living"; he stresses that the patients' coping reactions are learned from social stereotypes of crazy behavior. Following the societal reaction, Szasz states, treatment personnel label and reinforce the "crazy" stereotypes by the nature of their interactions with the patients.[2]

2. Thomas Szasz, "The Myth of Mental Illness," pp. 113–18.

Proponents of the labeling school such as Goffman, Szasz, Scheff, and others have little empirical evidence to support their view that social labeling causes insane behaviors.[3] Labeling theory generally places blame for mental disorder upon society and specifically upon treatment agents. Ironically one of the supporters of this theoretical orientation provides evidence against labeling as causative of the disorder; Denzin shows that patients' misbehaviors occur prior to the first patient-doctor contact and therefore, by implication, the disordered behavior could not have been initially created by the treatment contact.[4]

Sociologists have not been alone in placing blame for mentally disordered behavior on treatment personnel or on authority figures in society; many psychiatrists, since the 1930s, have looked toward the family and interpersonal dynamics as a causative factor in mental illness. Recently some psychiatrists have joined the labeling school of sociologists in attacks against psychiatric treatment structures while downplaying the part that personality or disordered behavior plays in patients' difficulties.

Labeling theory provides an ideology to assist in pressing for reforms of the treatment system. These views are, unfortunately, only partially correct. In an effort to combat custodialism, incarceration, and the stigma attached to mental disorders, many critics neglect to look at the negative aspects of the patient's primary behaviors in the social system and, especially, in the home.

Families who commit patients or who refuse to take patients home are often portrayed as rejecting, as shirking economic responsibility, or simply as dumping the patient on the state. Treatment personnel in mental hospitals are accused of brutality, cruelty, and callousness in their efforts to control patients. In essence, the special nature of patient behavior, for example, the aggression, the bizarre, and the destructive aspects are glossed over in an eagerness to avoid endangering reforms directed toward developing community-oriented care.

In the following section problems in the behaviors of patients at home are examined in detail. This focus on the patient's problem behavior turns out to be quite predictive of the patient's treatment ex-

3. Erving Goffman, *Asylums*; Thomas J. Scheff, "The Societal Reaction to Deviance: Ascriptive Elements in the Psychiatric Screening of Mental Patients, in a Midwestern State," pp. 401–13.

4. Norman K. Denzin and Stephan Spitzer, "Paths to the Mental Hospital and Staff Predictions of Patient Role Behavior," pp. 265–71.

periences and helps to clarify the nature of schizophrenic behavior, familial reaction to it, and the reasons for patient hospitalizations.

Study Group Comparisons on Problem Behaviors

A 22-item problems subscale was included in the SO interview schedule for use during the original ITC intake and thereafter at regular intervals with the home care patients. The checklist provides the SOs' descriptions of the patients' behaviors at home and difficulties caused by patients in the household. High problems scores are consistent with patients' rehospitalizations. Table 19 in Appendix D presents a comparison of the patient groups on problems behavior at the follow-up in 1969.

The three groups do not differ significantly from each other on the total problems score; the mean score of the drug group is 28.01, of the placebo group 26.24, and of the controls 28.77. There is no significant difference on 18 of the 22 individual scale items; for instance, 45 percent of the drug group, 46 percent of the placebo group, and 40 percent of the control group are described as uncooperative. Forty-two percent of the drug group, 38 percent of the placebo group, and 37 percent of the control group cause their SO difficulties because they are constantly talking and are restless. Of the control group 40 percent are problematic because they behaved oddly, as are 34 percent of the drug group, and 37 percent of the placebo patients. None of these differences reach statistical significance. The same pattern obtains for all of the remaining 18 items on the 22-problem checklist; the groups do not differ measurably on the individual items nor on the total problem score. These findings support the hypothesis that the three groups are not to be differentiated from one another five years after ITC's termination. It also highlights the continuing problematic behavior of these patients over a long period of time.

There are four problem items of the 22 on which group differences were statistically significant. These are: (1) the patient is a strain because he is dependent upon others; (2) he upsets the household routine; (3) he causes the SO a lot of worry; and (4) he requires excessive attention. In each case it is the controls who are the most problematic group. In the previous chapter the data showed that controls tended to be the least educated and among the economically dependent upon aged parents; given these characteristics it is possible to interpret why they are more problematic on these items.

Rank Order of Problem Behaviors

The totals column in table 19, Appendix D, presents problem behavior in the rank order of difficulty created for the SOs. Forty-four percent of the SOs state that the patients are not cooperative and, as we shall see, this becomes a major item in explaining many of the relational difficulties of schizophrenic patients.

The next ranked problem is talking and restlessness reported by 39 percent of the SOs; fourth are complaints about the patients' odd speech and odd ideas, reported by 37 percent; and fifth, 35 percent of the SOs cite patients as problematic at nighttime. Continuing down the list, one finds that patients are a strain due to their having to be watched excessively, that SOs fear what patients might do, and that these combinations of problems create strains upon family members. More than 20 percent of the SOs say that patients worry them because they fear that the patient might harm himself, that the patient complains excessively about physical problems, and ultimately that patients upset the household routine and are a physical strain on the SO.

Complaints (see table 19, Appendix D) that percentage-wise only average 13 to 19 percent are: children are ashamed of the patient mentioned by 19 percent of the SOs whose patients have children, and worry that the patient might harm someone else cited by 17 percent. Sixteen percent of the SOs are upset about the patients' sexual behaviors, 16 percent say that their children fear the patient, and 13 percent are personally afraid of the patient. Even though these problems are reported by relatively few SOs the nature of the problems is serious and they demand more than ordinary consideration. Behavior involving potential harm to other persons should carry a higher priority than a problem such as excessive talking.

In sum, the most frequently cited and most problematic aspects of patients' behaviors are bizarre ideation, speech, and action, and the fact that when upset the patients are noncooperative and cause SOs worry about the patient's well-being. An upset patient does not sleep well at night, hence entire households may be upset for 24 hours at a time, leaving SOs emotionally and physically drained. The facts add to an understanding of why families rehospitalized patients.

Longitudinal Comparisons on Problems Behavior

In table 20 in Appendix D the problems behavior of each group is compared at the original ITC intake to behavior at six months under

ITC care and with behavior at the follow-up in 1969. Scores for the six-month ITC evaluation period are available only for the drug and placebo home care groups; checklist data were not collected at, precisely, the six-month interval for the control group.

An important finding is that larger numbers of patients are reported as problematic at the time of ITC intake than are so described at any other time period. Conversely, when original ITC intake percentages are compared with those at six months the impact of drug therapy upon the home care drug group is once again obvious. On 16 of the problem items, percentages of SOs citing difficult behaviors decreased by two-thirds over the intake percents. There was a decrease from 48 percent of the SOs citing uncooperativeness as a problem to only 4 percent after six months of ITC home care time.

The placebo group's scores also decreased during the original home care study, but the improvement was once again less dramatic. On only 10 items did percentages for placebo patients drop by as much as one-half; the change was not as great as the two-thirds drop on 16 problems for the drug group. Scores on reported problems for placebo patients generally decreased by only a few points between ITC intake and the six-month period. This pattern demonstrates the comparatively greater impact of drugs upon the home care drug group as well as the continued higher rate of disturbed behavior of placebo patients. Nonetheless, it is possible to marvel at the effect that ITC home care had upon the reduction of problems among placebo patients who were not receiving active medications of any kind. Such a finding reinforces the perspective stressing the importance of aggressive socio-supportive home contacts that include the entire family group in therapy.

In table 20 (Appendix D) particular note should be taken of the comparisons at the six-month interval of the original ITC study with the follow-up data in 1969. Looking at the figures for the home care drug group on all items, the percentage of SOs who report problem behavior increases between the six-month interval and the follow-up evaluation. For example, the percentage reporting the patient as uncooperative increased from 4 percent during ITC to 45 percent by the time of the follow-up; on the item of excessive talking and restlessness the figures were 9 percent at six months with an increase to 42 percent by the follow-up; a similar pattern prevailed on the majority of other items. Evidently the cessation of ITC home care coincided with an increase of problem behavior among the home care drug patients. This finding agrees with reports in Chapter 3 regarding the increases in psychiatric symptoms for drug patients between the end of ITC care and the follow-up in 1969.

The placebo group, in contrast, as shown in table 20 (Appendix D) reversed the pattern of the drug group. On 12 of the 22 problem items placebo patients improved in their reported behavior following the cessation of ITC care, the time period during the follow-up in which most had received medications. Twenty-seven percent of the placebo patients were reportedly upsetting the household routine after six months under ITC care whereas at the follow-up only 11 percent were cited as problematic; 56 percent of the placebo group caused the SO worry at the six-month period but only 35 percent continued to do so by the follow-up. The most plausible explanation for this improvement was that placebo patients benefited from the initiation of outpatient drug care after the termination of the ITC placebo experiment. Drug care benefited this group more in the post-ITC period than the purely socio-supportive care received during the ITC experiment. This is a reconfirmation of findings in Chapter 3.

Rank Order of Problems

Table 21 (Appendix D) presents the rank order of problems most frequently cited by SOs at ITC intake compared with the follow-up. The first, third, fourth, and fifth ranked problems at follow-up were among the top five problems at ITC intake. The problem behaviors were: (1) causing the SO a lot of worry, ranked one at intake and one at follow-up; (2) odd speech and odd behavior, ranked two at intake and four at follow-up; (3) talkativeness and restlessness, ranked four at intake and three at follow-up; and (4) causing trouble at night, ranked three at ITC intake and five at follow-up.

The next five problems interchanged in rank order but were among the top ten problems cited during both time periods. These behaviors were: noncooperativeness; overdependence; worry about the patient's safety; upsetting household routine; and excessive physical complaints. The most evident fact is that problems that distressed families are repetitive and consistent, the same problems created difficulties for families at both evaluation periods showing a continuity in interpersonal problems and the kinds of difficulties presented by schizophrenics over time.

The four most mentioned and most difficult problems are intrapsychic in nature; in other words, they reflect psychic difficulties such as odd speech, odd ideas, making constant noise and talking, and restlessness. These data provide a graphic emphasis upon the bizarre nature of mental disorder as well as the patient's resultant noncooperativeness with his family. This serves as a reminder that patient rehospitalizations are in reality linked to disordered behavior, behavior that is difficult for families to handle.

Domestic Performance

As stated earlier in this report the poor task performers are not always those in need of rehospitalization for emotional distress. Angrist's research on mental patients demonstrates that female patients "exhibited 'similar' profiles on domestic role performance to the profiles of normal women."[5] On the other hand her research also demonstrates that the normal women are somewhat the better domestic performers and are clearly better adjusted psychiatrically.[6] To date, we are seemingly in the position of saying that psychiatric patients perform more poorly as a group, but that poor domestic performance is not a necessary concomitant of psychiatric distress nor is it always predictive of a need for rehospitalization.

Instrumental performance factors must therefore be regarded as variables that differ in nature from those assessing either rehospitalization or treatment experiences. As a measure of domestic performance we have a performance scale used in many of the prior studies on mental patients. This scale has been reported as fairly reliable; but it is nonetheless our opinion that the scale could be more adequately developed to test a wider range of domestic functions.[7] Further it could be improved by the removal of unclear items such as the following: Did the patient solve daily problems? Did she plan daily activities? Did she do other shopping? These items detract from the specificity of the scale and from its ability to distinguish low from high performers. Disturbed persons are able to get through a day "solving problems" and "planning their own time"; perhaps even wandering out to the corner store. Emotionally disturbed patients participate in such activities sufficiently well to suit their limited abilities. Family members rarely offer consistent help in "problem solv-

5. Angrist et al., *Women After Treatment*, p. 161.
6. Ibid.
7. Ibid.; Pasamanick, Scarpitti, and Dinitz, *Schizophrenics in the Community*, p. 95; Freeman and Simmons, *The Mental Patient Comes Home*, p. 54; (also see Appendix B).

ing" or in the preparation of a daily domestic work schedule, but they do have to assist patients in the performance of specific household tasks. Such evaluations of nonspecific task items are therefore highly subjective exercises and the scale would be improved by their removal.

Domestic Performance at Follow-up (1969)

Table 22 (Appendix D) demonstrates that the groups, drug, placebo, and control, by follow-up do not differ significantly in the proportion of patients who assume housekeeping duties and who act as homemakers, or who spend the majority of their time as a homemaker. Forty-four percent of the home care drug group are primarily homemakers, as are 51 percent of the placebo patients and 42 percent of the control patients. These differences are not statistically significant. Similarly nearly equal percentages of the drug, placebo, and control patients are considered physically and mentally able to do the housework. Also comparable percentages of women in each group are the primary homemakers in the household. Our assessments of domestic performance continue with the understanding that the study groups are alike on the availability of women in each group to do housework tasks.

Of five out of eight of the task items on the domestic performance scale, see table 6, the control group's performance is significantly poorer. Fifty-three percent of the drug patients are able to clean the house without help, as are 53 percent of the placebo patients, but only 37 percent of the controls are able to do this; the difference is significant at the .05 level. Forty-eight percent of the drug patients can cook meals without assistance, as can 49 percent of the placebo patients, but significantly fewer of the controls can do so, only 39 percent of them. On laundry and "other shopping" tasks the control group is also less able to perform adequately.

On tasks such as budgeting, paying bills, planning daily activities, or solving daily problems group differences near statistical significance at the .01 level; the controls' performance remains poorer than that of the other two groups. Domestic scale totals also demonstrate this tendency; the controls have the poorest mean score total, 16.56, the placebo group 19.14, and the drug group 19.24; differences near statistical significance at the .10 level of confidence.

The controls' poorer performance might be explained by the fact that almost twice as many of them are considered by their SOs to be

TABLE 6

DOMESTIC TASK PERFORMANCE OF WOMEN
AT FOLLOW-UP (1969)
(In Percent)

Domestic Task	Drug Group N=35	Placebo Group N=29	Control Group N=34
Cleaning house	53.2[b]	52.8[b]	37.2[b]
Cooking meals.	48.3[a]	48.8[a]	39.3[a]
Laundry and cleaning	52.3[a]	54.3[a]	30.8[a]
Grocery shopping	48.9[a]	53.2[a]	35.4[a]
Other shopping	57.8[a]	64.3[a]	38.7[a]
Budgeting and paying bills	38.1[c]	43.8[c]	30.8
Planning daily activities.	62.9[c]	58.0[c]	53.8
Solving daily problems	54.3	56.4	45.8
Total domestic performance mean score	19.24[c]	19.14[c]	16.56[c]
Caring for children[d]	29.1	26.8	19.0
Rated as a poor parent[d].	17.3	18.4	13.8

[a]Significant at .01 level of confidence.

[b]Significant at .05 level of confidence.

[c]Nears significance at the .10 level of confidence.

[d]N's for patients with children, drug group (26), placebo (19), and controls (18).

"too mentally ill" to do the housework (table 22, Appendix D); 19 percent of the controls are so considered versus 11 percent of the placebo and 9 percent of the drug patients. Recalling table 1 in Chapter 1 and table 17, Appendix D, the controls are the least likely to be married and are the most dependent on parents; these facts assist in explaining their low performance levels. Other research has reported that patients living with parents are poorer performers than those living with spouses.[8] Low expectations in such households reinforce poor performance on the part of the patient.

Longitudinal Comparisons of Domestic Performances

Table 7 presents a comparison between patients' domestic task performances during ITC and at follow-up. The pattern found was that

8.   Freeman and Simmons, *The Mental Patient Comes Home*, p. 93; Angrist et al., *Women After Treatment*, p. 161.

TABLE 7

DOMESTIC TASKS ON WHICH PATIENTS NEEDED HELP AT THREE TIME PERIODS
(In Percent)

DOMESTIC TASK	DRUG GROUP			PLACEBO GROUP		
	ITC Intake N=37	ITC 6 Months N=33	Follow-Up N=35	ITC Intake N=29	ITC 6 Months N=24	Follow-Up N=29
Cleaning house.	52.8	34.5	46.2	42.3	37.5	46.5
Cooking meals	50.0	25.9	51.8	40.7	35.7	51.3
Laundry and cleaning. . . .	47.1	29.6	48.1	32.0	37.5	46.2
Grocery shopping.	55.2	36.0	50.9	45.5	35.7	35.8
Other shopping.	43.8	23.1	42.2	32.0	35.6	35.7
Budgeting and paying bills	50.0	40.0	61.8	43.5	30.0	55.7
Planning daily activities .	61.8	16.1	37.1	32.1	22.2	42.1
Solving daily problems. . .	62.9	23.3	45.5	40.7	17.6	41.7
Total domestic performance mean score.	13.8	16.4	19.0	15.9	15.2	19.3

home care drug patients performed poorly at ITC intake, improved after receiving ITC care and worsened in the follow-up period. At intake 53 percent of the home care drug patients were unable to clean their homes without help, after six months of care only 35 percent needed help; by the time of the follow-up the percentage needing help had increased to 46 percent. Similarly at intake, 50 percent could not cook meals without assistance; after six months of care only 26 percent needed help, but by the time of the follow-up the percentage needing help had increased to 51 percent. In general (see total mean scores, table 7) home care drug patients showed an overall poorer performance at the follow-up than they had at ITC home care intake! This is in diametric contrast to the trends noted on psychiatric status or problem behavior, which were poorest at ITC intake when all patients were simultaneously having psychotic episodes.

The placebo patients improved between ITC intake and the six-month period of ITC home care, but improvements were generally not so marked as those seen in the drug patients, a finding attributed to the lack of active drug medication that hindered the placebo patients' overall improvement during ITC. Comparing follow-up performance to the six-month ITC home care evaluation of the placebo group, they regressed on domestic task performances at the time of the follow-up; in fact their performances, much like the home care drug patients, were poorer than at ITC intake.

The control patients' scores on domestic functioning were not available for the six-month ITC home care evaluation, hence this group was not included in table 7. Their scores, from our data, nonetheless showed that their performance at follow-up, like that of the placebo and drug patients, was poorer than at ITC intake. Their mean total domestic performance score was 14.0 at ITC intake and was 17.1 at the follow-up. Eight of the nine task items showed the deterioration of domestic task performance abilities between ITC intake and the follow-up in 1969.

Looking at the performances of the patients collectively a majority of the domestic task items show increasingly higher percentages of disabled patients at the follow-up; to be precise this happens on 16 of the 24 comparisons possible in all three groups. This pattern differs from findings on mental status and on the problems checklist variables in which patients' scores worsen after ITC home care terminates (excepting placebo patients) but never become *worse than at the original ITC intake.* Even the scores of the placebo patients, with post-ITC medical care, worsens on domestic performance. Thus it appears that regardless of the form of treatment over the follow-up the domestic performance of patients shows a tendency to deteriorate.

Why domestic performance should become increasingly poorer with time and why task items should respond less to psychiatric care than the patients' mental statuses is not exactly clear. The answer may be related to the process of aging as it results in the debilitation of physical motor abilities. It is also possible that once patients are relieved of the responsibilities for task performances the opportunity to resume them is not given at a later date. Broken familial ties also operate to reduce task demands and the ITC patients, throughout our years of study, had moved toward fewer such marital relationships.

Vocational Performance

The percentages in table 8, for all groups, on the vocational and economic variables are largely self-explanatory and in this very self-explanation are disheartening. It is clear that at follow-up time the men have almost no occupational identity; few of them, a little over one-fourth, had *ever* established an occupation. Twenty-seven percent of the male drug group have listed an occupation, 26 percent of the males in the placebo group, and 27 percent of the controls. Most of the men are not sufficiently identified with a work role to be listed, even, as common laborers.

Between 23 and 39 percent of the males in each cohort are welfare recipients. Most of the patients' welfare checks are based on mental disability and almost a third more in the placebo group than in the other groups receive such grants (27 percent of the placebo patients versus only 15 percent of the drug group). This higher recognition by welfare agencies of mental disability in the placebo group is due to the fact that during ITC home care the project's social worker secured financial grants based on emotional disability for the patients; placebo patients who were in greatest mental distress were in the greatest need of financial help. Once approved such disability grants are seldom reviewed and are seldom revoked.

Between 1964 and 1969 few of the male patients worked continuously either part-time or full-time, only 18 percent of the drug group, 9 percent of the placebo group, and 9 percent of the controls did so.

TABLE 8

VOCATIONAL PERFORMANCE OF MALE PATIENTS
AT FOLLOW-UP (1969)
(In Percent)

Vocational Item	Drug Group N=22	Placebo Group N=11	Control Group N=14
Identifies with an occupation.	27.3	25.7	26.7
Welfare recipient.	23.4	38.7	23.9
Vocational level improved in post-ITC period.	1.2	1.3	1.3
Vocational level dropped in post-ITC period.	25.4	36.8	25.0
Continuous employment in post-ITC period.	18.0	8.9	8.5
Officially designated as disabled	15.0	26.7	17.4
Disabled (official and SO designated combined)	27.7	48.8	31.9
Unable to get hired.	25.0	19.6	10.9
Seeking work (1969).	1.9	7.8	7.7
Job lost because of mental difficulties	16.7	15.8	25.9
Patient is main breadwinner.	44.8	52.8	43.1
Household income $3,500 or less. . . .	37.8	43.9	44.3

Major reasons for the poor work histories lie in the patients' mental conditions; 15 to 17 percent of the patients were officially receiving grants for mental disability and an additional 13 to 22 percent were considered too sick to work by other family members (see table 8). Of this latter group it is felt that many more would have received disability grants if a social worker or similar professional had taken the time to guide and follow patients' disability applications through the complex of official red tape.

Another 11 to 25 percent of the SOs stated that patients could not get hired, yet fewer than 9 percent of the patients in either group were seeking employment, a fact that belied the patients' stated interests in getting a job. Only 2 percent of the drug group, 8 percent of the placebo group, and 8 percent of the controls were seeking employment. Poor work histories and long psychiatric treatment records were prohibitive and contributed to the nonproductivity of patients. One of the most damaging figures is that of those who had worked, 17 percent of the drug patients, 16 percent of the placebo patients, and 26 percent of the controls lost jobs because they had emotional episodes, interpersonal troubles with co-workers, or performed jobs poorly because of mental problems.

Looking at the bottom of table 8 other facts may be noted; half of the patients are the main financial support of their families, 45 percent of the drug patients, 53 percent of the placebo patients, and 43 percent of the control patients are the chief breadwinners. Depending as these patients do upon disability welfare assistance or upon common laboring skills, average yearly household incomes are very low, under $3,500 for many patients. This finding highlights the serious implications for patients, families, and society of the financial burden of mental disorders; this regardless of whether patients are hospitalized or in the community.

Table 8 shows that, at best, only 1 percent of the patients has improved vocationally since ITC intake; conversely 25 percent of the drug group, 37 percent of the placebo group, and 25 percent of the controls dropped in their vocational levels. Evidently, the groups performed increasingly poorly during the time period from ITC inception to follow-up. Male patients do as poorly in the vocational areas as female patients do in their domestic task performances. In essence both males and females in all groups deteriorated in social task performance between ITC intake and the follow-up.

The data on vocational performance suggest two conclusions: first, the drug, placebo, and control groups do not differ significantly after the termination of ITC (this is supportive of hypothesis two); second, the patients in all groups worsened occupationally since ITC intake, and this supports hypothesis three. Male patients are poor vocational providers and females poor housewives; an accumulation of hospitalizations, emotional upsets, and increasing age adversely affects task performances, and task performance abilities decreased over time with little respect to treatments patients receive.

Social Participation

Social Activities at Follow-up (1969)

The last area of community functioning to be examined is the patients' social behaviors. Table 23 (Appendix D) presents the results of a comparison of the three study groups on an array of social activities. The major finding is that the groups, at follow-up, do not differ measurably on any of the social participation variables. During the course of the original ITC home care study the quality of social functioning shows a tendency, although not significant statistically, to be related to the patients' psychiatric condition. By the time of follow-up differentials due to treatment groupings disappear as do the variances in patients' psychiatric statuses (see Chapter 3). These results place social participation among the variables supporting hypothesis two.

Table 23 (Appendix D) shows that patients have considerable difficulty with social activities; between 35 percent and 49 percent, depending on the group, have no close friends, a fact explainable by some of their unpleasant social habits. Thirty-three to 47 percent of them can not meet people without acting strangely, one-fifth of them have embarrassing or bizarre eating habits, another 20 percent are messy and strange in their appearances. Poor judgement with money is fairly commonplace; 33 percent of the drug group are inadequate in money matters, as are 31 percent of the placebo group and 29 percent of the controls. Since patients' habits are peculiar they often refuse to eat with the family or what the family members eat; so they often eat alone.

Patients' activities remain limited to passive entertainments, watching television, listening to the radio, and sitting around with the family. They do not belong to organizations or to clubs. When they go out, they go with family members to visit other family members. Their average scores on the social participation scale range from 19 to 21 points. A very active person with a maximal social participation scores can receive a score of 10, a totally inactive person a score of 30; patients' scores are in the low-20 range. Very few improved their social participation scores once ITC terminated.

Patients' Living Situations at Follow-up (1969)

The former patient groups, as shown on table 9, do not differ significantly in their living situations by follow-up. Eleven percent of the drug group live alone, 7 percent of the placebo group, and 17 percent of the controls; differences are not statistically significant. By the follow-up between 7 and 17 percent of the patients are living alone whereas at ITC intake the requirements for acceptance into the study stipulated that patients had to live with their families. These data emphasize that a number of patients have severed familial ties between the original ITC intake and the follow-up study period.

TABLE 9

PATIENTS' LIVING ARRANGEMENTS AT FOLLOW-UP (1969)
(In Percent)

Living Arrangement	Drug Group N=57	Placebo Group N=41	Control Group N=48
Alone	11.4	7.3	16.9
With spouse.	43.2	36.4	36.8
With parents	16.0	19.5	20.4
With children.	11.4	14.8	0.0
With relatives	5.3	6.4	6.3
Group situation.	7.9	8.7	6.8

Forty-three percent of the drug group live with a spouse, as do 36 percent of the placebo group and 37 percent of the controls; these differences are not significant statistically. Comparing the percentages of those married at the follow-up to those married during ITC (see table 10), between 7 percent and 19 percent of the patients have divorced since ITC and in each group there are 3 percent to 6 per-

TABLE 10

SOCIAL BEHAVIOR OF PATIENTS AT FOLLOW-UP (1969)
COMPARED WITH ITC INTAKE (1962)
(In Percent)

Social Behavior	Drug Group N=57	Placebo Group N=41	Control Group N=48
Social activities score improved since ITC intake	1.0	8.7	3.6
Friendship pattern same to worse since ITC intake	59.9	51.0	58.7
Divorced or separated since ITC terminated	19.4[b]	6.6[b]	12.5[b]
Has married since ITC terminated . . .	13.4[a]	3.7[a]	7.7[a]
Remained single (lifetime)	28.4	51.3	39.3
Psychopathology caused changes in close familial ties since ITC terminated	27.9	23.3	17.9

[a]Differences significant at .05 level.

[b]Differences significant at .01 level.

cent more who have divorced than who have married, leaving more patients divorced when all of the shifting is completed by the end of the follow-up. The differences are significant with the drug groups' patients having experienced the most divorces. Nineteen percent of the patients in the drug group have divorced since ITC, as have 7 percent of the placebo patients and 13 percent of the controls. Thirteen percent of the drug patients have married since ITC, as have 4 percent of the placebos and 8 percent of the controls; the drug group's patients are statistically significantly the most likely to have married since ITC.

A plausible explanation for this higher activity in the drug group rests on the nature of the impact of ITC care; during the study the staff worked hard in the homes with the families as well as with patients to alleviate problems. Social and familial support probably acted to preserve marital situations but when the inhibiting, or helpful, eye of ITC was withdrawn patients' marital relationships deteriorated. Thus, home care drug patients were more eligible to marry over the follow-up for more of them had divorced after ITC terminated.

Relationships with the Opposite Sex

To provide insights and explanations about patients' interpersonal relationships, the project director, along with each patient's nurse, using information given by the SO, discussed and judged the degree to which a patient related in a pathological manner to members of the opposite sex. Behaviors termed abnormal were: avoiding the other sex completely, homosexuality, promiscuity, or bizarre sexual indulgences. Figures for each of those judged pathological are, for the drug group 39 percent, for the placebo group 35 percent, and for the controls 37 percent. It is the researchers' opinion that a central problem of schizophrenia is the disturbed person's inability to form a sexual identity or to handle sex-related roles; this view is congruent with most psychoanalytically based theories. Accepting such a perspective necessitates seeing the schizophrenic disorder as a pervasive problem in living, in that, socially, sexual role identification is at the core of personal identity in most societies of the world.

Social Behaviors Viewed Longitudinally

The majority of the patients have remained status quo in or have deteriorated in their ability to make and relate to friends or to preserve their marital relationships. Sixty percent of the drug group's relations with friends are the same or worse than at ITC intake, as are 51 percent of the placebo patients and 59 percent of the controls. Only a negligible percentage of patients have been able to improve their social activities scores since ITC intake, 1 percent of the drug patients, 9 percent of the placebo patients and 4 percent of the control patients (see table 10).

Data (see table 10) on relational pathology are deduced from information compiled on familial changes since the end of ITC. Household changes precipitated by the patients' interpersonal problems with either males or females are therein represented. This measure serves to substantiate what is already known about patients' difficulties in interpersonal relationships; 28 percent of the drug group altered familial ties over the follow-up period because of personal pathology, as did 23 percent of the placebo group and 18 percent of the controls.

Findings on social variables suggest: (1) that the study groups do not differ significantly, one from another, by the time of follow-up (with the exception of the excessive divorce and marriage rates among home care drug patients), once again offering basic support to the second hypothesis; and (2) that, in regard to social adjustments, patients do not (with very rare exceptions) show any improvement; this result provides support for the third hypothesis.

Conclusions

Patients' records on community adjustment are poor. The project director rated all patients on their ability to perform their major sex role using as a basis for the rating a combination of domestic, vocational, and parental performance variables. The percentages in each group whose performance is judged to be either fair to poor are 43 percent of the drug group, 51 percent of the placebo group and 52 percent of the controls. The differences among the groups are not significant statistically. Patients have recurrent psychiatric episodes and become disabled as marital risks, as social participants in community affairs, as vocational workers, homemakers, and even as friends.

Looking over the findings in this chapter the situation is less positive than that provided in the previous chapter that dealt with patients' treatment experiences. The drug, placebo, and control groups do not show the same consistency and rank order of debility on performance variables as they had shown on the psychiatric and mental status variables. For instance, the patients did not uniformly enter ITC with their poorest adjustment, improve after ITC care, and then get worse by the follow-up evaluation. The trend on vocational and domestic task performance is that patients became progressively worse over time regardless of the treatment received.

Considering that a psychiatric illness is either a personality based and/or an organically based problem, we may expect measures of mental states to be more consistent and direct than measures of socioenvironmentally related behaviors such as community adjustment. Measures covering times, days of hospitalization, or the IMPS psychiatric index are direct expressions of patients' mental states and are therefore more consistent with patients' mental illnesses than the variables in this chapter based on social factors. Social adjustments depend upon social structural, psychological, and interactional factors; in short, a multitude of factors impinge upon and neutralize community adjustments. Emotional upset affects task performance but the effect is not direct or so consistent as that noted on mental status measures or on the problem behavior variables.

Patients, when viewed as a unitary group, show consistely poor community performance. They do best in the less structured and stressful area of social participation. They fail noticeably in competitive situations such as the economic and public job spheres; the majority are either dependent upon welfare, upon a spouse, or upon a parent for their economic survival. Their vocational inabilities are reflected in low socioeconomic statuses and low family incomes. Interpersonally and maritally they fall far short of making satisfactory adjustments and are more likely to live alone as time passes. Community performance levels of patients are poor during ITC and they remain in status quo or, even more frequently, deteriorate over time.

chapter five

Successess and Failures

It will be recalled that all members of the ITC sample were schizophrenic patients admitted to the area's public mental hospitals com-
mencing in 1961. All were between the ages of 18 and 62, were
neither homicidal nor suicidal, and were expected to live with their
families. The vast majority of the families were willing, when asked,
to cooperate with the treatment plan. The study population was a
near complete representation of all schizophrenics, meeting the above
requirements, who were admitted to the public hospitals in Louisville during the two-year study period. Since it has been demonstrated in the previous chapters that the ITC project had no statistically significant lasting effects, this patient sample may now be
treated as a single group abandoning the drug, placebo, and hospital
control categories.

In this chapter an attempt will be made to distinguish between
patients who stayed out of the hospital during the follow-up and
those who did not. The former shall be classified as *successes* and
the latter as *failures*. The nature of patients' problem behavior in the
family, as well as the relationship between psychic states, task performance, and social functioning will be explored from this perspective. In this manner we can explore those characteristics that distinguish patients able to avoid hospitalization from those who are
hospitalized.

Characteristics of Successes and Failures

Table 11 gives the demographic characteristics of successes and failures. The only statistically significant difference, beyond the .05 level, among the variables is that the successes are more likely to be married. Fifty percent of the successes are married compared to 33 percent of the failures. Additionally, nearing significance at the .10 level of confidence: 60 percent of the successes are women as opposed to 73 percent of the failures, and 24 percent of the successes are black versus 39 percent of the failures. Low statistically significant differences (at .10 level) were also found in patients who kept the same SO as during ITC, 77 percent of the successes and 61 percent of the failures had the same significant other over the follow-up. Also at the .10 level more successes, 71 percent versus 53 percent of the failures, were economically self-reliant. It is quite possible that some

TABLE 11

SUCCESSES AND FAILURES COMPARED ON
DEMOGRAPHIC CHARACTERISTICS
(In Percent)

Characteristics of Patients	Successes N=61	Failures N=85
Female	60.0	74.3[a]
Black.	24.4	39.1[a]
Mean age[c].	42.9	42.0
Married.	50.4	33.4[b]
Catholic	27.3	18.2
Has same SO as during ITC. . . .	76.9	60.8[a]
High school graduate	35.3	28.4
Welfare recipient.	34.3	27.3
Patient is economically[d] independent.	71.3	53.4[a]

[a]Difference approaches significance at the .10 level.

[b]Difference significant at the .05 level.

[c]In years.

[d]Patients were considered economically independent if they were not reliant upon relatives (other than a spouse) for income, therefore some patients who were welfare recipients were categorized as economically independent.

of these differences would have proved to be statistically significant at the .05 level if the number of cases in this study had been larger.

A number of the demographic variables appear to reflect the better psychiatric condition of the successes including such variables as the stability of a marriage, continuity of the SO, and economic independence. As we have previously suggested, these variables are often linked to psychiatric or emotional well-being. Other research, dating from the time of Durkheim's work on suicide, shows that being married has an impact upon stability; conversely it is probably true that the less stable do not remain married or never marry in the first place. The two characteristics sex and race, however, cannot be the results of a psychiatric state. Nonetheless, it is possible that femaleness and blackness, we well as being divorced or single, constitute undesireable statuses and that occupants of them encounter more negativism and emotional strain than do their counterparts: the whites, the males, and the married.

Patients' Mental Statuses

Earlier in this book, in the conclusions to Chapter 4 and elsewhere, it is stated that the patients' psychiatric conditions coincide closely with treatment histories, and now it is possible to present more evidence on this point. The Lorr Psychiatric Inventory, as answered by the SO during the follow-up, indicates that the hospital failures are significantly sicker than the successes.

In table 12 the data show that there is a significant relationship between psychiatric factors and rehospitalizations. The successes' mean score on paranoid ideation is 4.40 and the failures' score 8.93; the difference is significant at the .01 level. The successes' mean score on hostile agitation is 1.22 and the failures' 2.16; this difference is significant at the .05 level. On feelings of depression the successes average 1.46 and the failures 2.32; this difference is significant at the .05 level of confidence. On perceptual distortions, thinking disorganization, and bizarre speech the same pattern prevails. Finally, the total weighted score is 13.02 for the successes versus 22.93 for failures; this shows that the successes are mentally healthier (the statistical difference is significant at the .01 level of confidence). Significant differences are also evident on the subscales: excitement-retardation, thinking distortion, and the schizophrenia score. Three psychiatric-symptom items fail to show significant differences, retardation,

TABLE 12

PSYCHIATRIC INVENTORY MEAN SCORES OF
SUCCESSES AND FAILURES

	Psychiatric Scale Factor	Successes N=61	Failures N=85
A	Excitement.	1.46	2.11
C	Paranoid ideation	4.40	8.93[b]
G	Bizarre motor behavior.	1.87	2.82
H	Hostile agitation	1.22	2.16[a]
E	Feelings of depression.	1.46	2.32[a]
F	Perceptual distortions.	.30	1.04[a]
I	Retardation and apathy.	1.44	1.87
J	Grandiose ideation.	.48	.76
K	Thinking disorganization and bizarre speech.	.44	1.14[b]
D	Disorientation.	.03	.07
	Total weighted score.	13.02	22.93[b]
	Excitement-retardation	2.08	3.07[a]
	Perceptual and thinking distortion . . .	5.16	10.53[b]
	Schizophrenia score.	3.62	5.88[a]

[a]Statistically significant beyond the .05 level.

[b]Statistically significant beyond the .01 level.

grandiose ideation, and reality orientation (all of which have relatively low rates of occurrence), and even on these the successes are rated as less disturbed than the failures.

Problem Behaviors

Table 13 presents findings that describe the differential in problem behavior at home between successes and failures. The most evident fact about the data is that 9 items are significant beyond the .05 level. The total-problems score differential is significant beyond the .05 level. The hospital failures are significantly more problematic; 45 percent of them cause trouble for their families at night, versus 25 percent of the successes. On worries about the patient hurting himself, 40 percent of the families of failures express this fear versus 13 percent of the families of successful patients. Some behavior is such that the families feel that patients would hurt other people; 25

TABLE 13

BEHAVIOR PROBLEMS REPORTED BY SIGNIFICANT OTHERS:
PERCENTAGES OF SUCCESSES AND
FAILURES EXHIBITING THEM

Problem Behaviors of Patients	Successes N=61[a]	Failures N=85[a]
Troublesome at night	25.3	45.2[b]
Nursing problem.	10.2	17.9
Safety causes worry.	12.8	40.0[b]
Causes worry about safety of others. . .	8.0	25.3[c]
Uncooperative.	37.4	54.3[c]
Strain due to dependency	30.8	31.9
Talkative and restless	26.1	51.4[b]
Excessive physical complaints.	18.4	29.2[d]
Sexually rude and improper	11.0	22.1[c]
Speaks and behaves oddly	22.8	52.3
Causes trouble with neighbors.	10.2	22.5[d]
Upsets household	10.4	24.8[b]
Upsets social life	16.3	19.7
Causes absence of others from work . . .	2.1	7.4
Causes children's absence from school. .	.0	7.2
Causes SO a lot of worry	34.7	65.4[b]
A physical strain on SO.	16.2	29.7
Requires excessive attention	21.0	32.4
Children are ashamed of patient.	5.2	10.1
Children fear patient.	2.8	9.2
SO is ashamed of patient	5.4	13.2
SO fears patient	8.3	19.2[c]
Total problems score (Mean)	25.42	30.35[c]
Having problems with alcohol	35.4	37.7

[a]N's for patients with children were 28 for successes and 35 for
failures.

[b]Statistically significant beyond the .01 level.

[c]Statistically significant beyond the .05 level.

[d]Approaches statistical significance at the .10 level.

percent of the families of failures worry about this versus 8 percent
of the families of successes. The failures are significantly more uncooperative with family members (54 percent versus 37 percent of the
successes). The same pattern of significant differences prevails
throughout including such problems as: excessive talking, restlessness, sexual rudeness, obnoxious behavior toward other people, and
oddity of speech and behavior.

Some items do not significantly differentiate successes from failures: (1) the dependency problem; (2) the nursing problem (neither group is a problem in this manner); (3) the physical complaints that create a strain on the SO (both successes and failures are troublesome this way); (4) the need for excessive attention (common to both successes and failures); and (5) the disruption of familial social activities (which happens, to a minor degree, in both groups).

The data show that bizarre behavior is primarily responsible for problems at home and later, as we shall see, for precipitating rehospitalizations. Over 50 percent of all failures are reported as exhibiting odd behavior, restlessness, and excesses in speech. Psychiatric distortions in thinking processes cause the patients to be noncooperative and to have poor sleeping habits; all of these problems create excessive worry among SOs regarding the patient causing difficulties for someone else. Forty percent of the failures' families worry about the patient harming himself; 23 percent worry about the patient causing trouble with the neighbors. Nineteen percent of the SOs worry about the patient harming them. Given the patients perceptual thinking and emotive distortions, bizarre behavior, inability to cooperate with others, and the resultant fears of the SO for his own and others' safety, it is not difficult to see why families seek hospitalization for such patients, and why they become failures.

Hospital Treatment Histories

This section presents a review of patients' previous treatment experiences. The question under consideration is: Are the current failures those with consistently poor or long hospital-treatment histories prior to this follow-up? Concurrently we will consider the persistence and stability of patients' mental disorders over the years.

Table 14 presents seemingly contradictory data for it appears that the failures have the poorest record during ITC home care on the number of times hospitalized as well as on the amount of time in the hospital. But, prior to the original ITC home care period the failures can not be distinguished from the successes in their hospital histories. Retrospectively, during ITC the successes average .65 hospitalizations, the failures .97 (this difference is significant at the .05 level). Successes average 1.5 months in the hospital during ITC and the failures 3.5 months; a difference significant beyond the .05 level. Yet, prior to the ITC study the successes were hospitalized 2.3 times and

TABLE 14

HOSPITALIZATIONS PRIOR FOLLOW-UP
SUCCESSES COMPARED WITH FAILURES

Hospitalizations	Successes N=61	Failures N=85
During ITC		
Mean number of times hospitalized. . . .	.65	.97[a]
Mean months of stay.	1.50	3.50[a]
Prior to ITC		
Mean number of times hospitalized. . . .	2.3	2.4
Mean months of stay.	11.4	13.1
Lifetime		
Percent in hospital over 10% of lifetime	8.3	18.4
Percent hospitalized three or more times	36.4	63.5[b]

[a]Statistically significant at the .05 level.

[b]Statistically significant at the .01 level and beyond.

the failures 2.4 times; this difference is not significant. Prior to the
original ITC home study the successes spent 11.4 months, on the
average, in the hospital, versus the failures' 13.1; again a nonsignificant difference.

There are two ways in which the fact that failures had poorer histories during, but not before, ITC may be explained. First, it is probable that one's recent past affects current behavior and explains it
better than the distant past. The period prior to ITC, is the most distant from the follow-up and thus proved less predictive of the patients' statuses at the post-ITC home care evaluation. Secondly, prior
to ITC data, hospital histories were dependent upon SOs' abilities
to recall the information during an interview; conversely the hospitalization data during ITC were recorded from hospital records by
the researchers and probably were more accurate.

Looking at the lifetime hospitalization figures in table 14 it is apparent that 64 percent of the failures had extensive rehospitalizations
versus only 36 percent of the successes; also, the successes spent less

of their lifetimes in hospitals. In general our data indicate that the failures had the more extensive treatment history, but the further back in time one goes the less predictive are hospitalization experiences for patients' present statuses; also there is less of a lifetime at risk for hospitalizations in the earlier time periods.

Clinic Treatment Histories

It is a general assumption among practitioners that outpatient clinics serve, or at best ought to serve, as preventative facilities for patients; with this fact in mind we present the following data. Surprisingly, as shown in table 15, it is the failures and not the succes-

TABLE 15

CLINIC TREATMENT OF SUCCESSES COMPARED WITH FAILURES
DURING THE FOLLOW-UP, 1964 TO 1969

Clinic Care	Successes N=51	Failures N=75
Mean clinic contacts.	14.2	16.0
Mean days of care	582.0	696.0
Percent of time, when not hospitalized, in clinic care.	37.2	41.3
Percentage never attending clinic	50.4	34.4[a]
Percentage attending clinic, over 90 percent of nonhospitalized time.	24.1	15.3

[a]Statistically significant at the .05 level.

ses who are most likely to attend outpatient clinics during the follow-up years. Of the successful patients 50 percent never attended the clinic but among the failures only 34 percent were nonattenders; this difference is significant at the .05 level of confidence.

Other findings are not significant although they support the trend which indicates that failures are the clinic attendees. The mean number of contacts for the entire follow-up period for the failure patients is 16 versus 14 for the successes. Of the total follow-up time period the failures average 696 days and the successes 582 under clinic care. The failures also spend a slightly higher percentage of their eligible (i.e., nonhospitalized) follow-up time under clinic care; 41 percent versus 37 percent, respectively. Upon closer analysis of this data we find that numerically more failures attend clinic for briefer periods of time; in short, the pattern of clinic usage differs. Although fewer successes attend, those who do go regularly and for longer periods of time. Clinics are used by patients seeking help after the onset of their emotional problem; they are used more for acute treatment rather than as preventive care centers. For only a small minority of patients does clinic treatment play a preventive role; 24 percent of the successes versus 15 percent of the failures attend clinic regularly (for over 90 percent of their nonhospitalized follow-up time). In sum, clinics are used by those who are emotionally disturbed in attempts to ward off rehospitalization. Some successful patients, a minority, use the clinic for supportive purposes. In general, the utilization of clinic services is more of a negligible variable in effecting success in avoiding rehospitalization than we had anticipated.

Differentials in the Use of Outpatient Clinics

Explanations for the outpatient clinics' infrequent impact on the course of patients' illnesses are presented in table 16. A major factor

TABLE 16

RELATIONSHIPS AMONG PATIENTS, FAMILIES, AND CLINIC--
SUCCESSES AND FAILURES COMPARED
(In Percent)

Relationship	Successes N=51	Failures N=75
Resistance explains nonattendance.	22.2	30.3
Patient is uncooperative	10.3	21.5[a]
Family is uncooperative.	13.0	31.4[b]
Family members are problematic at home.	29.3	58.4[b]
High psychopathology among family members.	19.2	51.5[b]
Good overall use of clinic program by patient	39.9	26.5[b]
Clinic program well suited to patient.	30.8	21.0[b]

[a]Statistically significant beyond .05 level.

[b]Statistically significant beyond .01 level.

in clinic use is the patient and family cooperativeness with the clinic. Analyzing only the attenders, patients who had some clinic contact, the emotionally healthier successes and their families are significantly more cooperative with the clinic's personnel. Twenty-two percent of the failures are rated as noncooperative versus 10 percent of the successes. Noticeably, only 13 percent of the successes' families are uncooperative compared with 31 percent of the families of failures. Differences in these two variables are significant beyond the .05 level of confidence. Noncooperativeness does not differentiate successes from failures in time spent under care, but family noncooperativeness prevents the failures from receiving maximal benefit from clinic programing.

Data in table 16 show that family pathology is more evident in the homes of the failures as are concentrations of familial problems. Fifty-eight percent of the failures have families that are problematic most of the time compared to only 29 percent of the successes. Over half, 52 percent of the failures' families exhibit extensive pathology versus only 19 percent of the successes' families. As one might anticipate, the problematic and sick patients live in problematic and disordered homes.

During the original ITC home care study it was learned that medications were essential to the prevention of hospitalizations; our follow-up clinic data helps to highlight this important fact. Attendance at clinic is not always related to the prescription of, or the taking of, medications. A number of patients receive either no medication or reduced drug dosages per clinic doctors' orders, some discontinue their drugs against medical advice, and other patients receive renewable prescriptions that they refill with minimal or no medical supervision. Data show (see table 24, Appendix D) that in comparable periods 31 percent of the successes are taking a regular and stabilized dose of medication while only 2 percent of the failures are doing so.

The emergent pattern from the composite information is this: the successes, when attending the clinic, make maximal use of the facility by cooperating, attending regularly, and taking medication regularly; the clinic in turn responds with appropriate programing. The pattern of care for the failures is less desirable. They and their families are less cooperative and more likely to miss appointments; they take their medications irregularly, if at all; and the clinic's program, in turn, is less suited to them. All of the preceding points to the need for aggressive home care visitations as a mode of involving the less cooperative families and patients in continuing outpatient medically supervised care.

Precipitants of Hospitalization

Table 24 (Appendix D) presents as a major finding that intrapsychic, cognitive, perceptual, and emotional problems dominate and are the primary accompaniments of hospitalizations for failures. Intrapsychic factors are the most cited prehospitalization events (this factor is chosen when the patient is upset emotionally and absolutely no other stress or problem, external to the patient, is apparent). All of the failures experience overt psychic upsets before hospitalization whereas 13 percent of the successes have no apparent problem or upset during a six-month comparison-observation period. An interesting perspective is to note the relatively *low* number of successes that are stress or problem free (13 percent)—reinforcing the fact that schizophrenia continues as an ongoing psychic problem even for those avoiding hospitalization.

Of interest is the fact that interpersonal problems are more likely to be experienced by the successes, 26.9 percent exhibit them during the six-month observation period; failures show fewer problems of this type prior to hospitalization, only 18.3 percent do so. This is understandable due to the social isolation of the sicker patients. Physical health problems and social-structural stresses such as economic problems, deaths, and job losses are insignificant factors during the observation period for both the failures and the successes. Failures do experience more cumulative problems, for example, two or more combined stresses, than do successes. Regarding types of problems experienced, the findings chiefly show that intrapsychic difficulties, occurring without any apparent external precipitant, precede hospitalizations. These findings offer little support for the view that socio-environmental stresses are major precipitators of psychotic episodes. Our findings agree with results in Langner and Michael's work, *Life Stress and Mental Health,* in which they find no evidence that lower-class persons experience more stresses than those in other social classes; hence there is no support for the belief that poor socioeconomic conditions create more stress and therefore more mental disorder.[1] In agreement also are the results of the initial ITC study in

1. Thomas S. Langner and Stanley T. Michael, *Life Stress and Mental Health: The Midtown Manhattan Study.*

which the concomitants of rehospitalization are found to be predominantly bizarre, aggressive, or destructive behaviors; in other words, psychic disorder.[2] Findings indicating that intrapsychic problems are the major event prior to rehospitalization are also present in the work of Angrist and her colleagues.[3]

We therefore continued to be confronted with the perplexing problem that emotional upsets are not clearly related to social stress or problem factors in the environment. We have yet to find a way to measure or assess the manner in which the normal or the mentally ill perceive or interpret their life conditions or events as problematic. The possibility exists that individuals interpret events as problematic quite differentially, some observing threat where others may perceive none. Also it is fully possible, as our data would lead us to believe, that psychic upsets are triggered by physiological mechanisms irrespective of external environmental factors.

Economic and Vocational Factors

Neither patients' personal incomes nor their abilities to work appear to bear as much of a relationship to success or failure as we had expected. On a majority of the vocational variables there is no significant difference between the successes and the failures.

Table 25 (Appendix D) shows that 62 percent of the successes list no vocation versus 64 percent of the failures; other patients simply do not have a work identity. After the ITC experiment the successes did more poorly vocationally than failures: 37 percent of the successes have a lesser occupation at the time of the follow-up than during ITC home care, but only 26 percent of the failures show such a loss. The successes showed this deterioration in their job statuses because they were more likely to hold jobs and therefore had something to lose.

Continuing with table 25, it may be noted that the successes are significantly less likely to be dependent on someone such as a parent, sibling, or child: 87 percent of the successes versus 74 percent of the failures are normally reliant upon themselves or a spouse. Other findings demonstrate that successful patients tend to be vocationally competent, but not significantly so.

2. Pasamanick, Scarpitti, and Dinitz, *Schizophrenics in the Community*, p. 106.

3. Angrist et al., *Women After Treatment*, p. 162.

Differences generally lack statistical significance on the vocational factor since both successes and failures are poor vocationally, both are lower-class persons, and relatively few in either group have a vocation or much of a work history. The successes had more vocational responsibilities and again ironically they dropped most in their occupational level in the post-ITC home care period.

The data show that successes do not differ significantly from failures in socioeconomic status or on the amount of annual, personal, or familial income (see table 26, Appendix D). The successes' mean score on socioeconomic status is 62.0; the failures' 64.0 (a nonsignificant difference).

More failures than successes, 32 versus 19 percent, respectively, changed their source of financial support between 1964 and 1969. More failures than successes, 81 percent versus 56 percent, have annual household incomes under $5,500. Also more failures than successes, 65 percent versus 55 percent, have personal incomes under $3,500 per year. The failures are comparatively poorer, their families are poorer, and they have been poorer for a longer time.

In sum, successes score slightly higher on the socioeconomic scale, are somewhat better educated, and are more likely to remain as breadwinners after ITC. The economic factors tend toward the direction of what one would expect them to even if they failed to be statistically strong differentiating variables.

Domestic Performance

In the domestic sphere the results are very much like those on vocational variables. With few exceptions there are no significant differences between the domestic functioning of the successes and the failures; once again, poor task performance fails to be clearly related to the psychic well-being or the hospitalization of patients.

There are, however, a few interesting trends and some significant differences of note (see table 27, Appendix D). The successes are less likely to be full-time homemakers, mainly because they work; 18 percent of the successful women work outside the home versus 8 percent of the failures. Conversely, the failures are more likely to be full-time homemakers, 75 percent of the failures versus 68 percent of the successes; at the same time they are also slightly less able to perform domestic chores.

Other researchers have shown that failures are more likely to have others in the home who can do their domestic work for them.[4] In our case 15 percent of the failures have domestic role replacements available versus only 6 percent of the successes. Interestingly more of the successful women carry a dual load, work and housework, with less help in the home, and they do a better job.

In two crucial areas significant differences between successes and failures occur. These are areas in which families are least likely to tolerate poor performance, the parental role and the handling of money. Our data show that 30 percent of the failures are unable to minimally fulfill parental responsibilities whereas only 13 percent of the successes are unable to do so (see table 27, Appendix D). This difference is significant at the .01 level of confidence. Not only are failures poorer parents but their parental abilities worsened over the follow-up period. On variables dealing with money-handling (see table 28, Appendix D) far more of the failures are unable to budget and pay bills, a difference significant beyond the .05 level of confidence. In two areas where performance is highly important differences are significant between the successes and the failures, that is, in the areas of child-rearing and money-handling.

Social Participation

On the social activities scale successes have an average score of 23.27 and failures a 22.93; this difference is not statistically significant (see table 29, Appendix D). Similarly 43 percent of the successes have poor social adjustments compared with 47 percent of the failures. Forty percent of the successes have poor friendship patterns versus 52 percent of the failures. No significant difference appears between the groups on changes in friendship patterns since the original ITC home care study. In brief, the social activities index does not differentiate between successful patients and those that are rehospitalized.

Marital and Familial Relationships

Patients' abilities to make and keep lasting heterosexual relationships are presented in table 30 (Appendix D); a number of the factors approach statistical significance and one is statistically signifi-

4. Freeman and Simmons, *The Mental Patient Comes Home*, p. 199.

cant. In essence: (1) failures are less likely to be married, 21 percent of the failures never married versus 13 percent of the successes; (2) successes are more likely to remain married (50 percent of the successes were married in 1969 versus 33 percent of the failures); (3) failures are rated poorer than successes on their ability to relate normally to the opposite sex; and (4) failures change their living arrangements because of emotional difficulties more often than successes.

As reported by their SOs, 58 percent of the failures relate in a pathological fashion to the opposite sex as opposed to 35 percent of the successes. There is a marked difference between the 16 percent of the successes who change their relational ties because of pathology and the 30 percent among the failures who do so.

Table 31 (Appendix D), which presents the patients' living situations at the follow-up in 1969, exemplifies the fact that most patients have interpersonal problems. More failures than successes live alone, 17 percent versus 5 percent. (At ITC intake none of the patients could live alone and qualify for acceptance into the study.) Fewer failures, 33 percent versus 50 percent of the successes, live with a spouse: relational patterns of the failures are less intimate and less normal given their expected age and sex roles as American society defines them.

Successes and failures move residences equally frequently. They both average 1.3 moves in the previous five-year period (table 31, Appendix D), but major differences are found in reasons for patients' moves. Thirty-seven percent of the successes move to improve their living conditions or for some other socially positive reason but only 20 percent of the failures move for equally legitimate reasons. Thirty-three percent of the failures move because of problems such as divorces, interpersonal difficulties, and conflicts with neighbors.

Conclusions

Therefore, in our search to understand why some patients are hospitalized and others are not we find that neither successes nor failures change as much as we might expect. The statuses of these patients during the ITC study program are generally maintained after the original home care study ends. The successes who are the better patients during the base-ITC study (as judged by hospitalization histories) continue to be the lesser hospitalized patients in the post-ITC period. In this manner we can say that a prior history of many hospitalizations is predictive of a future course.

Also, after ITC the failures, in comparison to successes, tend to do more poorly in their interpersonal relationships, change SOs more often, worsen as parents, and have somewhat poorer domestic performance scores. In short, failures tend to regress more than successes, but many of these variables, when considered singly, do not reach statistical significance and can not be used to predict future hospitalizations.

All patients, both successes and failures, did poorly vocationally, domestically, and socially after ITC ended. If they did not worsen, they simply remained in status quo at a low level of performance. The data provide added support for the third hypothesis showing that patients do not improve with the passage of time on performance variables.

The predictive variables show that successful patients are distinguishable from failures by: (1) their better mental states; (2) their less problematic behavior; (3) their own and their families' higher degree of cooperativeness with clinic care agents; (4) their more stabilized medical regimen; (5) their more frequent economic and vocational independence; and (6) their better adequacy in the parental role. It is probable that the better performances by the successes, when noticeable, are due to their better mental condition. It is also likely that the lesser cooperativeness of failures and their families with the outpatient clinics is due to their poorer mental states.

Recognizing that a patient's emotional state, as it affects his behavior, is interactive with other variables in his environment, such as vocational and economic successes, and that these achievements in turn bring improvements in mental states, we nonetheless are disposed to believe that the mental state is the most important explanatory variable and the pre-existing condition. Psychic, perceptual, and emotional problems are related to and are the most explanatory of rehospitalizations and clinic attendance. The psychic state, in turn, affects patients' adjustments in all spheres but is most significant in interpersonal relationships. The most disordered patients are surrounded by disordered families, whereas the healthier are living with less problematic and less disturbed families. It is probable that such families assist in the initial exacerbation of the mental illnesses; assuredly they help in perpetuating it.

chapter six

The Patients: Case Studies

This chapter is included in this book to serve as a reminder that real people, with a variety of difficulties, provide the substance of our study. The following case abstracts are representative of patient experiences and describe the interaction between differing treatment approaches, the varieties of schizophrenic pathology, and the differential in home situations of patients. We have deliberately included a few cases drawn from the original ambulatory ITC home care referrals whenever the cases are of unusual interest and demonstrate the factors we have found relevant in the careers of schizophrenics.

ITC Home Care Drug Success: Follow-up Success

Mrs. W., an ambulatory patient, was referred to ITC by the Louisville Area Outpatient Clinic. She was a 31-year-old, white, married female whose psychiatric history included four hospitalizations in both private and public facilities. She had, in the course of this prior care, received psychotherapy, electroshock treatment as well as drug and insulin treatment. Prior to her ITC referral she was on a regimen of ataractic drugs, but since she had failed to respond positively to them she was referred to ITC in an attempt to avoid hospitalization.

The family lived in a small, modest home in a lower-class neighborhood; the husband, John, was a man with two years of college education who worked as an office clerk; their son, Douglas, was four years of age. At referral time, Mrs. W. had numerous symptoms; for instance, she was obsessed with the idea that her teeth were shifting, and consequently she was unable to use her partial dental plate without experiencing severe pain; she also believed that her nose was changing. The psychiatrist's notes in the ITC medical record stated that she showed marked anxiety, difficulty in concentrating, fatigue, obsessive compulsive symptoms, depression, agitation, voluble speech, inappropriate affect, and had a definite thinking disorder. She showed limited insight into her symptoms and could offer no explanation for them. Her diagnosis was schizophrenic reaction, chronic undifferentiated type. A prescription of thioridazine (Mellaril), 100 milligrams, was given to be taken three times a day and tranylcypromine (Parante) 10 milligrams, to be taken once before bed time.

Prior to contact with ITC this patient had amassed numerous doctor and dental bills as she had gone from physician to physician seeking to alleviate her physical difficulties. At intake time, Mrs. W. sporadically talked about killing herself because she felt her discomforts could not be cured and because she believed she would never be attractive due to her changing facial features; she repeatedly requested shock treatments because she despaired of ever getting better. One day she confided to the ITC nurse that her uterus was out of place and was causing her considerable pain, her menses were irregular, and she expressed a repeated preoccupation with sexual matters. Her beliefs about her appearance and body, as well as her feelings regarding the futility of her situation, were repeated to the nurse hour upon hour in a whining and childlike voice.

Slowly and over repeated home visits the nurse learned about Mrs. W.'s childhood. She had grown up in a very poor rural Kentucky home in which most of the family possessions were purchased from Sears and Roebuck catalogues. Mrs. W. seldom discussed her mother, but about her father she said, "he never liked me and I was unable to please him." Her most serious complaint was that her father had not been willing to spend money to have her adolescent buck teeth corrected by a dentist. She often looked at the Sears catalogues, staring at the beautiful girls, wishing that she could look pretty like them.

After graduating from high school she left her home to enter nurses training; upon completion of the course she earned a degree as a registered nurse. While in school she met a boy from a nearby army base and a romance followed involving sexual relations. The boy-friend left for active duty promising to return for her, but he never did so. The young woman was bitterly disappointed and told her nurse that she felt her subsequent problems were due to that un-happy love affair. Shortly after that romance she married an old high school boyfriend, her current husband. Mrs. W. stated that she had never loved him and frequently, throughout the home care program, she repeated this assertion.

At the very beginning of home visits the nursing notes described the same repetitious pattern. Mrs. W. whined and complained about her physical problems, and she continued to dwell on the fact that she never expected to get better. She repeatedly consulted dentists and was preoccupied with her partial bridge; in fact, she would file on it and adjust it, spending an inordinate amount of time working on the bridge. Also, she would occasionally mention suicide; her hus-band, in response, would immediately call ITC and ask permission to commit her to a psychiatric hospital. Whenever the home situation became this problematic, the husband was asked to bring Mrs. W. into the clinic to talk with the psychiatrist, and the ITC staff's efforts were redoubled in attempts to encourage Mrs. W. to continue taking the medication and to advise husband and wife to be satisfied with a minimal level of adjustment. The staff always projected the belief that Mrs. W. would get better in the future.

During home care there were other chronic difficulties. Mrs. W. was a heavy smoker and drank up to half a bottle of whiskey per day. Her husband was very much opposed to these habits and would nag his wife, trying to prohibit her indulgences, but his demands were of little avail. The nurse also noted that Mrs. W. was unable to take adequate care of her home and she required her husband's constant help. The patient openly avowed a dislike for housework and this, when added to her psychic preoccupations, produced an inability to perform her tasks adequately. She was also unable to control or care for her young boy, who was so pesty and troublesome during home visits that the nurse nicknamed him "Dennis the Menace."

As home care progressed the ITC nurse despaired of being able to reach Mrs. W. or of comprehending the basic fears that resulted in her repeated obsessions with bodily changes. After months had passed, the nurse slowly became aware of an important fact: Mrs. W. was able to function more adequately whenever her husband or an-other family member was ill. During the early part of her marriage she had competently cared for a father-in-law with cancer and was also, currently, able to cope with most medical emergencies in the home, despite the problems in other spheres of her life. Furthermore, when forced to interact with neighbors and friends, her demeanor, including her voice, would change and her self-presentation would improve markedly. It was by observing the above that the nurse was led to suggest to Mrs. W. that she go back to work part-time at the hospital. After repeated encouragements and reassurances, the patient secured a job in a hospital operating room (her specialty) and proceeded to work, at first for two days a week and later for three or four. Henceforth a gradual but consistent improvement in her behavior became evident and persisted throughout the home care period.

When ITC terminated in 1964, Mrs. W. was not formally referred to another outpatient clinic since it was felt that none were available that could cater to her special needs; she was in the habit of regulating her medications as she wished, something she had done continually throughout ITC. In short, it was felt she would probably not follow the mandates of any existing clinic program. The assumptions were, in fact, erroneous.

In 1969, at the time of follow-up five years later, the nurse revisited Mrs. W.; the patient had not been rehospitalized in the interim and her adjustment level appeared even further improved over that at the termination of ITC home care. Mrs. W. had voluntarily sought attention at the state hospital's outpatient clinic. A review of the clinic notes on Mrs. W.'s visits showed that the psychiatrist who saw her was analytically oriented and had probed into the psychodynamics of Mrs. W.'s relationships with her father and her husband; he proceeded to interpret these relationships as basically hostile in nature. Mrs. W. did not like this approach and stopped attending the clinic, giving the excuse that she did not like Orientals since she at one time felt she looked like one (the psychiatrist was a Philippino doctor). She later reentered outpatient care when a psychiatrist she liked went into private practice. She said of this second doctor that he was quite blunt in his interpretations and the truth hurt, but she felt it was honest and it helped her. From our knowledge of this second psychiatrist we would state that he was less analytically oriented and basically handled Mrs. W. in a more supportive, therapeutic fashion. We have in general found that supportive therapy is more successful with schizophrenic patients than interpretive or analytic endeavors.

The patient and her husband, over the follow-up period, had

moved to a more attractive house and the income from Mrs. W.'s hospital job assisted considerably in making the monthly payment. The joint familial income was $9,500 per year, which was much higher than the income in most ITC patient homes. Mrs. W. had improved her relationship with her son and was taking him out to plays and various places of a recreational nature. Her husband, who had always been easy going, likeable, and generally tolerant, had ceased to criticize her for her heavy smoking and drinking, even though she continued to drink up to one half a bottle of whiskey per day and sometimes consumed this amount before going to work at the hospital in the morning.

Mrs. W.'s personal appearance had improved over the follow-up years and her nervous mannerisms were less noticeable. She was able to admit that she loved her husband and believed that she had become lovable. She could not understand why her husband had stayed with her through all the years and believed that she would have really "fallen apart" without his support. Even though she would, on occasion, complain about her teeth and her nose shifting, she had decided that she could tolerate and live with her difficulties. She had abandoned ideas of suicide, saying that she thought it would be unfair to her husband and her child; also, as a Catholic, it was against her religion.

In sum, Mrs. W., from the time of ITC intake, was successfully maintained on medication, both during and after ITC. She also had available to her continued therapeutic sources of support, first the ITC nurse, then a private psychiatrist, both of whom gave needed encouragement. Most importantly, she had managed to return to work and successfully diverted her energies from her symptoms to tasks directed toward meeting the needs of other people. She was among the minority of our patients who were fortunate enough to have skills upon which she could rely, despite debilitating psychiatric symptoms. Mrs. W.'s husband earned a steady salary, assisted with housework, exhibited no serious adjustment problems of his own, and ordinarily provided her with the emotional support and attention she needed. This patient was able to enter into a cycle of positive reinforcement, therapeutically, in the home, and at work; importantly, she also continued on medications throughout the eight years of study contact. We feel she was, for these reasons, a home care drug success and remained similarly successful through the follow-up, managing to avoid rehospitalization or the recurrence of extensive psychotic symptomatology.

Home Care Drug Success: Follow-up Failure

Mrs. C. was first seen at ITC in 1962; she was referred from the state mental hospital where she had admitted herself voluntarily because of suicidal preoccupations. She was described by the ITC psychiatrist as depressed, preoccupied with death, and troubled by numerous physical difficulties. Her affect was inappropriate, and she admitted to hearing voices and to having visual hallucinations; her diagnosis was schizophrenic reaction, acute undifferentiated type.

At the time of referral Mrs. C. was a 21-year-old, white woman with no formal prior history of mental hospitalizations, even though she had been treated by her general practitioner for nerves. She was given medication, trifluoperazine (Stelazine), 2 milligrams, four times a day, assigned an ITC nurse, and was sent home to live with her common-law husband and their one illegitimate child.

The ITC staff nurse learned that Mrs. C.'s childhood was unhappy; she had feared her stepfather and despised her mother who had forced her to do all the housework chores and who, Mrs. C. felt, had never cared about her welfare. The family had been exceptionally poor and when the patient was 16 years old her mother arranged to "give" her to the local grocer (in marriage) in exchange for payment of the family grocery debt. The young girl was married to, and lived with, this 60-year-old man for four years, and she never forgave her mother for this arrangement. When the patient reached 20 years of age she ran away from her forced marriage and went to live with Mr. C., a man nearer her age. At the time of admission to ITC care she and her common-law spouse had one child; furthermore, since her divorce from her husband was not final, she was unable to marry her current partner. Living in common law worried her greatly and constituted the major issue at the onset of ITC home care. The problem worsened when it became evident that Mrs. C. was pregnant with a second child. The ITC nurse and social worker, with the help of a local priest, assisted Mrs. C. in securing her divorce, whereupon she was able to marry her spouse two weeks before the arrival of their second baby.

Other conditions in Mrs. C's life were also troublesome; the couple lived with the mother-in-law who did not offer to help the patient in any way with the housework and who persisted in making demands upon her son, the husband. Mrs. C. was continually physically tired, run down, pale, and fearful of another pregnancy; she obviously was in need of both physical and emotional support. Such help was not forthcoming from the husband, who was a very passive and nonverbal man. He failed to recognize any of his wife's symptoms as mental in nature, passing them off as physical weaknesses. Mr. C. earned a moderate income as a factory worker, but he spent a good part of his money on nights out drinking with male friends. Whenever he drank, he became physically and verbally abusive toward his wife. To compound matters, he never assisted around the home and he ignored the children completely.

Ultimately the family moved from the home of the mother-in-law, but their next apartment was infested with roaches that got into the baby's bottle, the ice box, and the patient's medicine—it was a deplorably poor facility. Shortly after this move Mrs. C. became pregnant and her fears and anxieties increased along with her schizophrenic symptoms. The ITC staff, and in particular the nurse, provided her with the only social and emotional resources she had. The nurse visited regularly, brought the medications, and insisted that Mr. C. take his wife to the doctors she needed to receive attention for her physical problems and for prenatal care. The nurses resourcefulness was often pushed to its limits, but given concerted effort ITC was able to prevent psychiatric rehospitalizations for the patient during the study period.

When ITC home care neared its close, it was evident that Mrs. C.'s adjustment was marginal, her symptoms had abated only minimally and she was in danger of losing any small gains that may have been made. She lived in continual fear of becoming pregnant, a situation she felt would drive her "nuts" (a sentiment that the staff felt was not completely devoid of the truth). Yet Mrs. C. was not without some positive attributes, such as her ability to care fairly adequately for the children and to do so despite her numerous problems. The housework was also handled with some ability despite limited family finances and poor housing conditions.

When ITC terminated, all efforts were made to provide Mrs. C. with ongoing social and psychiatric follow-up attention. The county public health nursing association was contacted and asked to visit her monthly, to check on her home environment, the children, and to talk with the patient, giving her whatever encouragement possible. An ITC referral was also sent to the state hospital's outpatient clinic and the first appointment arranged for her. In regard to the clinic appointment, the staff was apprehensive of Mrs. C.'s keeping it, primarily because her husband could not be relied upon to take her to the clinic.

Fortunately, for six to eight months after ITC termination two of the ex-ITC nurses worked at the state's outpatient clinic and they continued home visitations; in this manner Mrs. C. was given care approximating that which she had received during ITC. A half year later the state clinic discontinued all home visitation and, as expected, Mrs. C.'s husband neglected to take her in for her scheduled appointments; consequently she ceased receiving regular medications. The problems were compounded when the clinic was moved from the downtown area and located at the state hospital, 30 miles from the center of the city, a difficult place to reach.

Shortly thereafter Mrs. C. became pregnant once again and also had another severe psychotic episode; she was hospitalized for psychiatric reasons five months after the birth of that child. Shortly after discharge from the psychiatric hospital she was admitted to a general hospital to have a hysterectomy and thereafter was admitted, once again, for a hernia operation. Following these medical difficulties, another psychiatric hospitalization occurred. In the intervening periods she did not receive any psychiatric follow-up attention or medication.

Yet, by the time of the follow-up visit in 1969, five years after ITC termination, Mrs. C. was described by the nurse as looking somewhat better, although she was still moody, frail, and obviously in marginal physical health. Since she had had the hysterectomy she no longer worried about additional children, which was a relief to her, but she continued to fear that her health was bad and that she would have serious illnesses in the future.

The children were older and easier to care for; they appeared well attended to and happy. The family's home was also an improvement over their prior ones. Even though Mr. C. continued to drink, he was earning a slightly better income, which enabled him to move the family to this better home. Mrs. C. still lacked outside social or familial contacts; the mother-in-law continued to be disliked and to cause problems in the family. The patient had seen her own mother only once in the prior eight years, at a time when the mother, faced with surgery, requested the presence of her daughter; Mrs. C. made that single visit to her in the hospital.

Even though by the time of the follow-up the overall social situation appeared improved, it was felt that much of the difficulty in the prior years could have been avoided if appropriate outpatient attention had been available. For instance, Mr. C. had never been counseled sufficiently to begin to accept the emotional basis for his wife's problems. It was also thought that the two psychiatric hospitalizations, which totaled six months of time over the five-year follow-up, could have been averted if Mrs. C. had been receiving medications and outpatient attention. During the second psychiatric hospitalization the children had to be placed in an orphanage, which upset them, as well as Mrs. C.

This patient's case has been presented to illustrate the advantages of aggressive home care and continued medical supervision for those patients who need social support because they lack familial, financial, social, or emotional resources in their own homes, and to demonstrate the social disorganization that can occur when such treatment supports are withdrawn.

Home Care Drug Failure: Follow-up Success

This case offers an example of how it is possible to keep a chronically ill patient out of the hospital through the use of consistent and aggressive home care. Interestingly, in the case of Margaret H., the appropriate care was provided by the state hospital's outpatient clinic and not by the ITC home care program. ITC had failed to assess and work correctly with this patient's situation.

Mrs. H. was referred to ITC during the early days of the experiment when the staff was inexperienced and relatively naive about how to handle home care crises. Mrs. H. came from the state mental hospital where she had been diagnosed as having a schizophrenic reaction, schizo affective type. The psychiatrists evaluation at intake noted that she showed marked anxiety, difficulty in concentrating, fatigue, withdrawal, insomnia, and was markedly depressed. Her actions were slow and stuporous also, her affect was bland and inappropriate. She was given trifluoperazine (Stelazine), 5 milligrams three times a day, and was sent home under the supervision of an ITC nurse.

At the time of admission to ITC, the patient was a white 43-year-old housewife; she had a history of 11 previous hospitalizations, the first of which occurred when she was 24 years old. She was one of nine children, a junior high school graduate, had been married for 20 years, and had given birth to seven children. Three of the children were living with her; they were a son, age four, and daughters, aged 16 and 18. Following the birth of her last child, Mrs. H. had had a hysterectomy. Mrs. H., her husband, and their three children lived in a three-and-a-half room house. The husband worked as a grocery clerk for a weekly salary of $40.17.

Mr. H., the husband, was an aggressive and demanding person who was intolerant of his wife's problems; he felt they were due to laziness on her part. In the past Mr. H. was in the habit of taking his wife to the mental hospital and admitting her whenever she became a problem at home. Yet, as we shall see, it became possible, given an understanding of this family, to divert this pattern, avoid further hospitalizations, and at the same time to improve the tenuous adjustment the patient made at home.

The event that preceded the hospitalization prior to her referral to ITC was the death of an older son who drowned in a river while Mrs. H. was in a general hospital with one of her numerous physical illnesses. Each year thereafter, on the anniversary of her son's death, she became depressed. The overall environmental pattern in the home was continued stress, problems with the children, and repeated hospitalization for physical and psychiatric ills. Mr. H. not only denied the emotional difficulties of his wife but also was cold and unresponsive to his children; for instance, he would lock his girls out of the house whenever they displeased him. Such an event took place two weeks after ITC home care became active in the case. After an argument with her father, the eldest daughter ran away from home and left her mother, the patient, without any help or supervision during the day. Mrs. H. became increasingly agitated over her daughter's departure and would incessantly pace around the home both during the daytime and nighttime. She managed to do some minimal housework and somehow to handle the bare necessities of care for her four-year-old son. The other, 16-year-old, daughter, it should be added, had left home during the first week of ITC care to get married. Mrs. H.'s anxiety and disordered behavior increased in intensity until she was staying up all night cooking. She never left her home nor talked with friends or relatives, even when they came to visit her.

Within three weeks of her acceptance onto the program, Mr. H. called ITC and said that he was going to return his wife to the state hospital because he had gotten a second job and he could not watch her either during the day or the night time. The ITC psychiatrist and nurse responded by saying that they did not feel that Mrs. H. needed to be returned to the hospital and that they would not approve of his taking this step, but also could not prevent him from sending her back if he so wished. At this early date in ITC care the staff was unaware that they could avoid such returns by mandate, that is, refusal. Policies toward patient rehospitalizations later in the program became stricter and more prohibitive. Mrs. H. was returned to the hospital and therefore became an ITC home care drug failure.

Following a two-week hospitalization she was discharged and her home life continued much as before; a repetitive pattern of crises and emotional upsets. During the remainder of the ITC study time and over the five-year follow-up period that ensued Mrs. H. had the following difficulties: her son, at the age of six, was referred to a child guidance clinic since his behavior in the class room was highly aggressive and disruptive; the husband was incensed at the referral and refused to admit that his son had any problems; he would not take the child to the clinic. Six months later a daughter who had returned home once again ran away due to fights with her father. Four months later Mrs. H.'s father had a heart attack, and when the patient became upset over this Mr. H. refused to pay for her medication from the state outpatient clinic and threatened to return her to the mental hospital. Fortunately, Mrs. H. was under the care of a doctor at the clinic who knew the patient and her home situation quite well; he refused to approve her admission and she was denied hospital entry. The clinic psychiatrist made emergency visits to the patient's home to give her injections of medication and to talk with the husband, urging him to be more tolerant.

Some three years after the termination of ITC home care the patient was involved in an auto accident in which she injured her back; she was hospitalized, requiring rather extensive medical attention. Within one month of her medical discharge after the accident, Mrs. H.'s mother had an operation and at approximately the same time both of her daughters became involved in serious marital difficulties. Both girls had married unwisely and both of them had had illegitimate children. One son-in-law had been shot to death by a neighbor during an argument and when this daughter remarried she entered into a second problematic liaison. The other daughter was beaten and physically abused by her husband, who had a record of three years in the state penitentiary. While the daughters were involved in marital problems, the patient entered the hospital for gall bladder surgery. Throughout these socially stressful events the patient was seen regularly by the state outpatient clinic. All together, on three separate occasions Mr. H. took the patient out to the state hospital intending to admit her and on each occasion the hospital contacted the clinic physician who stated that the patient's medication could be increased and that she could be maintained at home; all admissions were refused.

At the follow-up period, five years after ITC had terminated, the patient was continuing under the care of the outpatient clinic. The nurse, upon her follow-up visit, found that conditions in the family had slowly improved for some of the following reasons. One of the daughters had returned home with her child and was providing the patient with some social companionship as well as with help in the housework. The younger son, although still manifesting problems in school, was not in as much difficulty as previously. One of the older sons had, meanwhile, finished training in a seminary and was ordained as a priest. This son's accomplishments served as a special source of pride and pleasure for the patient as well as for the husband. It also appeared that, since there were fewer familial problems and fewer problematic children to handle, Mr. H. was more relaxed and had mellowed somewhat. Both husband and wife were communicating better, with a greater allowance on Mr. H.'s part for permitting his wife to assert herself and to make demands upon him.

In short, the clinic had, by preventing rehospitalizations whenever Mr. H. became frustrated with pressure at home and with his wife, interrupted a cycle of impulsive destructive action in this home. Mrs. H., assured of the support and interest of the clinic staff, was slowly becoming better adjusted and showing fewer symptomatic schizophrenic reactions. This case illustrates how chronic schizophrenics who live in disordered and problematic homes can be helped by socially supportive attention and continued medical surveillance; particularly when such attentions are taken into the homes during crisis periods. The clinic care, in this case, was appropriate and managed to reverse a cycle of repeated personal psychiatric failure to one of moderately successful home adjustment.

Home Care Drug Failure: Follow-up Failure

The following case describes a situation in which neither the patient's pathology or the destructive familial interaction could be altered by ITC or by any other existing treatment intervention. It is also a case in which it is possible to witness the repetition of events and psychotic upsets that resulted in this patient's hospitalizations. Andrew R. was a 20-year-old, black, single male; he was referred to

ITC after a transfer to the state mental hospital from the city hospital psychiatric ward where he had been taken by the police on a warrant of arrest.

Andrew was living at home with his mother; his father had died from syphilis when the patient was quite young and his only brother, two years older than he, had drowned shortly before the patient's referral to ITC. Andy had tried desperately to save his brother, but had been unable to reach him in time; this event and recollections of it upset him periodically in the years to follow. Andy had quit school after ninth grade and had worked at a variety of jobs; his current work was as a truck driver for an industrial firm; a job he had held for two years. Since his mother subsisted on a small welfare check, Andy was the primary breadwinner in the home. This patient was quite personable and was able to keep jobs, a difficult feat for most of our other patients. Andy's earnings totaled between $80 and $100 per week and, due to his income, there was little financial stress in the home.

Andy's mother was a domineering woman who tried to keep a close rein on all of his activities. According to other members of the family, Andy had been a spoiled child whose immaturities, demands for attention, and uncontrollable temper tantrums errupted whenever he was unable to have his own way, a fact that soon became obvious to his ITC nurse.

Upon acceptance into the program we learned that Andy had, prior to hospitalization, been picked up by the police for "ranting and raving" on the streets and for threatening a neighbor with a pistol. He exhibited paranoid ideas and believed people were trying to kill him. Andy was able to state that the cause of his difficulties was within himself, but he couldn't explain what it was. The psychiatrist's diagnosis was schizophrenic reaction, chronic undifferentiated type. The doctor noted that Andy exhibited moderate anxiety, difficulty in concentrating, fatigue, withdrawal, some feelings of worthlessness, guilt, depression, slowed speech, and a flat, and inappropriate, affect. He was given a prescription of trifluoperazine (Stelazine), 2 milligrams three times a day.

The nurse felt that Andy was basically an immature person who was unhappy at home due to an ongoing conflict with his mother. But, when the nurse suggested that he move out of mother's apartment, Andy's reply was, "I don't see how anyone can leave their mother." Andy's relationship with his nurse was unpredictable; there were days when he was talkative, charming, manipulative, and cheerful, and other days when he was sullen, antagonistic, muttering about suicide, and refusing to talk with anyone. He was nonetheless faithful about taking medication and would call the clinic asking for a supply whenever he missed the nurse's home visit, which happened rather frequently. Andy also requested increases in dosage whenever he felt that he was getting upset and needed help; his requests were granted if, after an evaluation by the psychiatrist, they were warranted.

Andy had friends with whom he would spend time, seeming to enjoy their company, even though he was irascible and often undependable in these relationships. He frequently had fights with friends and with neighbors, which as often resulted in his being picked up by the police. On two occasions the ITC nurse and psychiatrist provided evidence of Andy's treatment status to the judge to help him out of court difficulties. On another occasion he was rescued from trouble with the draft board with whom he had failed to keep an appointment for a physical examination.

Despite his fights and escapades with the law, Andy was liked by the ITC staff and there was a general feeling that he was making an overall improvement, and was cooperating as best he could. One day Andy presented his nurse with an invitation to his wedding, stating that it would take place in a month. His girl friend was described by the nurse as a "swinger" who had lived with a number of different men and had two illegitimate children; she was currently pregnant with Andy's child. The nurse attempted to dissuade both Andy and his girl friend, Dale, from getting married, but they were convinced that everything would go well and they were "in love."

The nurse attended the marriage ceremony, after which the newlyweds and the wife's two children moved into the apartment with Andy's mother. Within a week arguments ensued between the mother and the wife. Dale, the wife, thought that the mother demanded too much from the patient and was continually making Andy run errands. She also complained that he failed to help her with any household tasks or with the children. In response to the discord, the mother stated that she was going to get married and that Andy and his family would have to move out of the apartment. Before they were forced to do so, other events intervened.

As Dale's pregnancy progressed, Andy became more nervous, anxious, and agitated. The ITC nurse tried desperately to talk with both the mother and wife, urging them to avoid putting excessive pressures on the patient since she felt he couldn't withstand them and would probably react by having another psychotic episode. At last Dale was admitted to the hospital and she delivered a baby boy. Andy eagerly anticipated her discharge, in what he expected to be a few days. But when the day for her discharge arrived, her doctor decided to keep her for yet another day. The disappointed Andy threw a fit in the hospital lobby; he threatened a fight with the doctor and said he would forcibly remove his wife from the hospital. After being ejected from the hospital, he got drunk and proceeded to create a row in his neighborhood, attacking and threatening a neighbor, and once again shouted that neighbors were trying to kill him. As anticipated, Andy was picked up by the police on a warrant and was hospitalized in the psychiatric ward at the city hospital and later transferred to the state mental facility. Andy therefore became an ITC home care drug failure.

He remained in the hospital for two weeks (a period of time that became a commonplace pattern in later hospitalizations). Andy appeared to like the protective environment of the hospital, feeling somewhat safe, in a place where he could avoid demands and regain his equilibrium. Upon discharge he returned to his wife and three children. Shortly thereafter the mother did marry and the couple were forced to locate their own home. His wife started a course in nurse's aide training at the city general hospital, finished the course, and ultimately secured a job as a nurse's aide.

Five years later, at the time of ITC follow-up, the nurse learned that the course of events in the intervening years had been turbulent. The marriage had not worked well; the couple constantly argued with one another, fighting in an immature way. For example, one time Andy was asked to take one of the children to the hospital because the child had a bad cold; this cold was subsequently diagnosed as pneumonia, which upset Andy considerably. Once again he threw a temper tantrum in the hospital lobby, which served to embarrass his wife, who was an employee at the hospital. Andy continued to drink and to get into many minor scrapes with the police.

Never during the course of the follow-up was Andy referred to, nor did he voluntarily seek, assistance at an outpatient clinic; as a consequence he received no medications at home after he left ITC care. A major crisis occurred when the couple was ejected from their apartment and put on the street for the nonpayment of the rent, even though both of them had an income and could have afforded to pay the bill. As a consequence of complaints from neighbors and school authorities, the juvenile court became active in their affairs because of complaints about negligent treatment of the children. At one point the court took the children out of the home, placing them in foster homes until Andy and his wife could settle their own lives sufficiently to care for them. Predictably, Andy became very upset at the authoritative action of the court, got beligerant, threatened neighbors and once again created a disturbance on the streets. He was taken, as a result, to the psychiatric facilities. On two other occasions (a total of three) he was hospitalized in the mental hospitals for similar reasons.

By the time of the follow-up in 1969, Andy and his wife had separated; they had mutually agreed that they could not get along together. Andy was under a juvenile court order to pay $25 per week support money to this wife, but since he did not do this faithfully the court remained actively involved in the case. Hospital records documented that, upon each hospitalization, Andy had ideas of persecution, was depressed, agitated, and had become inappropriate in his speech and affect—he continued to have very limited insight into his problems. Despite his numerous hospitalizations, he was never after discharge referred by the hospital to any outpatient facility for follow-up care.

The last time the ITC nurse talked with Andy he was once again in the state hospital and was looking forward to being released in a week. He told his nurse that he was getting a divorce and that within a month he was going to marry a white girl he had met in Chicago who really liked him. He felt everything would work out well because they were in love.

In sum, we believe that until preventive psychiatry develops some techniques to authoritatively take action to help patients like Andy to stabilize their home and social lives and at the same time maintain them on a medical regimen, there is no way to interrupt their patterns of repeated hospitalizations. Authoritative measures would infringe on a patient's liberties and, as yet, psychiatry does not use such an outpatient approach to treatment. In Andy's case aggressive action would include moving him out of the mother's home and the denial of current permission to marry or to rear children. As long as immature patients are unable to exercise their own controls, permissive approaches cannot be expected to succeed in interrupting their patterns of repetitive hospitalizations.

(It would perhaps be of value to remind the reader that our data did not produce a correlation between environmental stress and psychotic episodes for the overall study population. Even though this preceding case and others appear to show clear relationships between stress and upset, we were unable statistically to validate environmental stress as a necessary correlate of psychotic episodes or rehospitalizations.)

Home Care Placebo Success: Follow-up Success

The following case is illustrative of a minority of home care patients that received placebo medications and who, although psychotic at the time of ITC intake, managed to avoid hospitalization without medication, aided only by the ITC socio-supportive home contacts. By the conclusion of home care the high majority of placebo patients, 65.9 percent, had failed; the staff concluded that the ones that had been able to avoid rehospitalization tended to be somewhat stronger and perhaps were inherently less pathogenic than other placebo patients. Many of them had experienced only the single psychotic episode that resulted in their ITC referral. Among these patients, and including the case we are about to review, were a number that never received any medication during the follow-up and continued to remain successes. In general we attribute this to their youth and to their lack of a serious or long history of mental illness.

John was 18 years old at the time he was referred to the ITC home care program; he was a handsome blonde youth who had just graduated from high school. He was a musician, a drummer, who played fairly well and was employed in local bands as well as with some that traveled out of the state. During ITC home care John played drums for a six-month period at a rather exclusive nightclub featuring striptease acts.

This patient was referred to ITC from the city general hospital's psychiatry ward with a diagnosis of schizophrenic reaction, acute undifferentiated type. His predominant symptoms were anxiety, difficulty in concentrating, fatigue, withdrawal, insomnia, obsessive compulsive symptoms, depression, inappropriate affect, unsystematized paranoid delusion, as well as auditory and visual hallucinations. We learned that prior to his hospitalization John had become upset when he discovered that his girl friend was pregnant and the girl's mother began to exert pressure on John to marry her. In turn, the patient's mother was strongly opposed to this marriage, which resulted in a controversy with John caught in the middle. John was sent home on placebo medication believed by the psychiatrist and staff to be chlorpromazine (Thorazine), 50 milligrams, two times a day, and trifluoperazine (Stelazine), three times a day. He was assigned a nurse to visit him regularly at home.

John's family history was rather poor and showed that emotional and social problems were the norm rather than an exception. An uncle, the mother's brother, had died as a patient in a state mental hospital; John's eldest brother had been hospitalized twice for nerves in private psychiatric hospitals; this same brother had also been married three times by the time he had reached 30 years of age. A younger brother stuttered quite severely and was such a behavior problem at home and at school that he was sent away to a military academy in hopes that it would "straighten him out.'

John's mother and father had been married three times and divorced three times. Throughout our eight years of contact they did not marry again, even though they saw one another daily. The father paid board to his ex-wife and ate all of his meals with her; according to Mrs. S., he never stayed overnight, but went home to his mother, in whose home he lived. The father was gruff, abrupt, and a controlling man who drank rather heavily; his presence always signaled an argument, which was a chronic form of interaction between him and his ex-wife. Mrs. S., the mother, was a tiny, vivacious, and likable woman who controlled her relations with the husband and her sons in a seductive and manipulative fashion. She worked full time on an assembly line in a factory and had done so for years. Battles were commonly between the mother and father, but oftentimes the sons were involved. On one occasion John tried to intervene in a fight to protect his mother and the situation deteriorated into a physical fight with his father. At the onset of ITC home care, John felt that his father was to blame for the parents' marital problems and it was many years to come before he recognized that his mother was also at fault.

John related to his mother like a spoiled, irascible child who demanded service for his meals and for his clothing needs; his mother was seen as primarily existing to fill these needs. Although he earned a salary and paid his mother a minimal amount for room and board, his requests for physical care were constant and his mother readily complied with most of them. John was described by his mother as lazy, self-centered, and unwilling to help around the house; she complained that he had a poor disposition and would frequently lie to her if it was to his advantage; yet she seldom directly countermanded his requests.

John's major preoccupations were with matters of sex; he frequently talked to the nurse about his conquests and powers with girls. He was also highly fearful of doing anything that would injure his body; for instance, despite the nightclub atmosphere in which he worked, he neither smoked nor drank. He spent his free time working on physical fitness exercises either in his basement or at the local YMCA. He also had a rather inflated image of his abilities, believing that he was the best drummer in town. He wanted to play with a really big-name band that would prove to all the quality of his real talents. He was usually involved in "deals" that he believed would cause such jobs to materialize and bring him fame; these dreams never came true; eight years later he was still performing in the same local nightclubs.

On another occasion he attempted to join the Marines and play for their band; he was rejected due to his psychiatric history. At yet another time he failed college entrance exams that would have brought him a scholarship to study music at a local university. John also often talked to the nurse about marriage; he felt that a good wife would probably solve all of his difficulties but he did not think he could ever find a good woman. Most girls, he felt, were out to take what they could get and did not really care for men. He also believed that all of his family members had made very poor marriages and that he would be no different; he never seriously considered marriage over the eight years of our contacts with him.

At the inception of ITC care John was quite mentally disorganized—he was given placebo medication that he took dutifully and that everyone, including the staff, thought helped him. His relationship with the nurse vacillated, but he was generally haughty and self-occupied, and bragging a great deal about his sexual and musical achievements. The psychiatrist, shortly after intake, counseled with the pregnant girl friend and, although we have no record of the doctor's conversation with the girl, she and her mother ceased pressuring John for a marriage; John soon forgot about her and never saw the child she ultimately bore. The psychiatrist had meanwhile referred the girl to a private psychiatric outpatient clinic.

The home situation throughout ITC remained status quo, that is, disputes and discord prevailed. John continued to work and was generally pleased with himself. He had spells of moodiness whereupon he would retire to the basement and play his drums for hours on end, or when he would talk in a manic and irrelevant fashion with flights of grandiose ideation. When he became particularly irascible at home, or incoherent, his mother would talk about hospitalizing him, but these periods passed rather quickly and John managed to avoid commitment. When ITC home care terminated the psychiatrist felt that the only remaining symptom was anxiety and that John had improved considerably over his status at intake.

At follow-up time five years later, the nurse saw very little change in the situation. John continued to play in bands and also held periodic jobs with the Greyhound bus lines as a driver. He had been refused admission to the army on the basis of his psychiatric history, and he thought that this was peculiar given that he was considered sufficiently responsible to man a Greyhound bus with 50 people dependent upon him. His parents' relationship continued in status quo, though Mrs. S. had been hospitalized for a four-week period, for nerves, in 1967. She had also inherited funds from the estate of a grandmother, which helped to pay 35 percent of the house mortgage, allowed for some interior decorating, and some financial investments. This assistance appeared to help Mrs. S.'s general outlook and gave her a feeling of security.

In conclusion, John's status at follow-up was fairly like that at the time ITC home care terminated. Given the continuance of social conditions at status quo, we did not foresee John's succumbing to further psychiatric problems—of course, a status quo cannot be guaranteed. Since this patient was still immature, we also believed that, if he should marry, he would expect a wife to cater to his needs much as his mother had done; also, that such a step would be problematic for him.

This patient's psychiatric illness had not been lengthy or severe; further, he managed without medication throughout ITC and the follow-up; the only assistance he received was the social-supportive interest and intervention provided by a concerned ITC staff. Given the low level of psychopathology of his illness and the existence of a stabilized, albeit argumentative, home pattern, such brief supportive help had sufficed.

Home Care Placebo Success: Follow-up Failure

The following case describes a home care placebo patient that benefited from ITC home care because of the efforts of her nurse and who failed during the follow-up due to an unforeseen error on the part of the doctor at an outpatient clinic.

Caroline came to ITC as a referral from the state mental hospital; she was diagnosed by the psychiatrists as suffering from a schizophrenic reaction. Her presenting symptoms were depression, withdrawal, a preoccupation with cleanliness, and obsessive compulsive thought processes. Her earliest symptoms prior to her hospitalization were vague feelings of distress because familiar things were changing; for instance, she believed that the wall paper in her house was changing, whereupon she experienced an increasing level of anxiety and mental confusion.

Psychological testing could not be completed at the time of ITC intake because Caroline mumbled in inaudible monosyllables and was unable to complete either the verbal tests or those requiring motor skills. She was assigned an ITC nurse and was sent home, unbeknown to the staff, on placebo medications.

At the time of intake Caroline was 25 years old. She was living with her mother in a poorly maintained and small home in a town some 20 miles south of Louisville. Her father had died when she was 14 years old; she was the eldest of seven brothers and sisters. Caroline had helped raise her siblings, assisting her mother with the housework; she had also worked at various jobs outside of the home. At the age of 18 she abruptly stopped working, stating that she felt unable to cope with the demands placed on her. She experienced her first psychiatric hospitalization at that time, to be followed by the second seven years later, prior to ITC intake. Her brothers and sisters had, by 1962, left the home, married, or were self-supporting; all were doing well except Caroline. Prior to her second hospitalization she had been attending a night class at a local college and had also been taking a correspondence course, hoping to finish her college education so she could become a librarian.

Relatives often visited the home, but prior to intake the nieces and nephews got on Caroline's nerves and thereafter voluntarily reduced their visitations. Most of her high school friends had either moved away from town or had married and acquired other interests; in consequence, she lacked any friends of her own. Caroline had been the valedictorian of her high school class, president of her church club, and had even worked for a local town newspaper. But, in the year prior to the second hospitalization, she had withdrawn from most social activities and stayed exclusively in the house, leaving it only to attend class or to take an occasional walk with her mother.

Caroline's mother was a heavy set and rather unresponsive woman whose only show of emotion in the eight years that we knew her came at the time of the follow-up, when the nurse asked what changes she wanted most for her daughter. Her response was, "to be normal," at which time huge tears rolled down her cheeks. Mother had never remarried and she earned barely enough money to support Caroline, working as a domestic for other people. Throughout ITC home care the mother was usually anonymous, unobtrusively carrying on with her work in silence.

The ITC nurse described Caroline's appearance as drab; she never wore any make up, her hair was drawn back in a bun, and her dresses were nearly floor length. During the early part of ITC home care she stayed in the house all day long, did very little of the housework, and often did not bother to get up and get dressed during the day.

The nurse became involved with this patient, who had managed to evoke sympathy from most of the professionals that came into contact with her. Working diligently, the nurse would spend two or more hours talking on each home visit. Within six months the patient began to respond to the nurse; she dressed up for her visits and obviously looked forward to seeing her. By the time the ITC study terminated, the nurse and Caroline had formed a very good relationship and noticeable progress had been made. Caroline was walking out to stores and to the post office; she cleaned the home, and had begun to take pride in her appearance; also, she was once again enrolled in a correspondence course for secretarial work and was making simple attempts to function socially. Even though Caroline continued to be withdrawn and shy, her speech and affect were no longer inappropriate and she was obviously better than at ITC intake. We attributed the patient's improvement during the home care study to the nurse's psychotherapeutic efforts with her for she had received only placebos during this time period.

When ITC home care ended, visitations for Caroline were not interrupted for her nurse went to work at the outpatient clinic in that county and was able to continue regular contacts with her. Then, an unfortunate incident occurred, the only experience of this nature to our knowledge among any of the placebo patients. Although her referral to the follow-up clinic clearly stated that she was on placebo medication, the clinic psychiatrist mistook this to mean a "placebo dosage," and since he felt that the patient was not functioning opti- mally, he increased the assumed drug dose and gave her an increased amount of actual medication. Caroline had a reaction and, recogniz- ing her own symptoms as "odd," contacted the doctor and was hos- pitalized for four days to overcome her ensuing anxieties and mental disorganization. After a four-day hospitalization, which resulted in her being classed as a follow-up failure, she was discharged with an appropriate and adjusted drug prescription.

Some two years later all outpatient home visitations from clinics were discontinued and the nurse was no longer able to maintain contact with her, but by this time Caroline was well enough to enter into group therapy sessions at the outpatient clinic. She continued to function fairly well at home, going out to stores, doing some house work, and keeping up with her correspondence courses. Caroline had slowly improved over the years and aside from the clinical error had managed to avoid a recurrence of severe symptomatology.

In this case it has been possible to observe the benefits of suppor- tive home care without medicines and to witness some minor im- provement once drugs are added to the therapy effort. It is our feel- ing that psychotherapeutic care alone may have sufficed for Caroline, which serves as a reminder that in a minority of cases psychotic schizophrenics may benefit from psychotherapy. In the last analysis, the utmost benefit and the safest course for most patients remain medications, combined with variations of familially oriented socio- therapeutic efforts.

Home Care Placebo Failure: Follow-up Failure

The following case describes a woman with a lengthy and chronic schizophrenic history. This patient maintained a tenuous adjustment in the community only so long as she was taking tranquilizing medi- cation regularly. Her hospitalization during the follow-up period dramatically followed the withdrawal of all her medications by a clinic physician.

Mrs. D., a 42-year-old married woman, was referred to ITC by the state mental hospital; it had been her eighth psychiatric hospitaliza- tion. Medical records described the typical pattern of disturbed be- havior that preceded each hospital admission; she would become agitated and argumentative, threatening her husband, eldest daugh- ter, and neighbors with knives or pistols. Her husband and daughter were frightened of her and they would usually swear out a warrant of arrest and have the police pick her up to transport her to the hospital. Because the patient never admitted that she was disturbed, the husband confessed that calling the police was the only way he could cope with his wife when she became disturbed.

Upon admission to ITC care the psychiatrist reported that Mrs. D. was agitated, hyperactive, overtly suspicious, and was pressured in her speech. She said that people, and especially her neighbors, were talking about her; she carried on conversations with voices in a hallucinatory fashion. Her diagnosis was schizophrenic reaction, paranoid type.

Her husband, Mr. D., was a thin, pale, and nervous man who readily admitted that he was afraid of his wife; she had, prior to the last hospitalization, attacked him and cut his chest with a large kitchen knife. He said that he tried to handle her with "kid gloves"; even when she made him very furious he had learned to turn the other cheek. None the less, it was obvious that he would have preferred to have left his wife in the hospital since he felt that she was still quite disturbed. Despite his feelings, Mr. D. meekly agreed to try home care; the patient was placed on placebo medication (in accord with the random study design) and was sent home with her husband and her eldest daughter.

Aside from the patient's behavior, the ITC staff soon learned that there were multiple difficulties in this family. Mr. D. was also under outpatient psychiatric care; ten years earlier he had been hospitalized in a private psychiatric facility for his nerves and for problems with drink. He continued to take medicine for his nerves. Mrs. D. said that early in their marriage her husband had spent all of his money on alcohol and would bring his companions, men and women, home for drinking sprees. Mrs. D. continued to be suspicious of his behavior with other women—including neighbors. Mrs. D. said that her husband was very irritable and drank and smoked too much. In contrast, Mr. D. maintained that he only drank a beer on occasion and that his wife was very unrealistic in her suspicions about him.

The patient also had very little respect for her mother, whom she described as a dumb scrub woman; and she called her father a drunken street cleaner. She had two brothers; one had been continually hospitalized at the state mental hospital from the age of 23 years with epilepsy complicated by psychoses, and a second brother was physically disabled and was a known alcoholic. Mrs. D.'s youngest daughter had married and left home, but the eldest daughter, who was at home, fought with her mother continually; this daughter ultimately had to seek outpatient psychiatric attention because of her nerves.

The family atmosphere as the nurse soon learned was continually disturbed. Mrs. D. maintained a prolonged argument with and a continual attack upon her husband and daughter, both of whom tried to avoid encounters with her. Mrs. D. followed them from room to room accusing them of misbehaviors and, at her worst, she would flail out and attack them physically.

Shortly after acceptance onto the ITC program, Mrs. D. got into an argument with her neighbor and spent a good portion of an afternoon out in the yard screaming obscenities and threats at the woman. As a result, Mr. D., distraught and worn out from three weeks of coping with his wife, called ITC to report that over the weekend he had returned her to the state hospital. He said that he was sorry, but that he felt that she had come home too soon from the hospital and was not quite ready for home care. Mrs. D., due to placebo medications, about which we learned at the termination of the study, had remained in a psychotic condition throughout ITC's brief contact with her and we had been unable to contain her florid behavior.

At follow-up time, five years later, the ITC nurse returned to this home. She learned that Mrs. D. had been placed under clinic care after her ITC hospital discharge and that she had, in fact, functioned quite well for three years. She had been maintained for those years on stabilized and continued dosages of medication. The clinic team had also referred her to Bridgehaven, a halfway house for mental patients, the purpose of which was to: (1) get her out of the home, and (2) to provide her with some social interests.

For those three years she experienced no significant psychotic episodes, although she continued to be argumentative. She still distrusted her husband, accusing him of infidelities; she would call him at work and, on occasion, would go over to the dental laboratory where he worked as a technician and embarrass him in front of his boss. She was frequently unable to handle the housework and the daughter and husband had to take care of the chores. She was not capable of handling money and always overspent or spent foolishly. The eldest daughter remained in the home and was described as too nervous to marry; the younger daughter had escaped the home to marry years before; she avoided any contact with her parents, and seemed to be making a success of her marriage.

Despite Mrs. D.'s characteristically paranoid way of relating, she had, over the follow-up, stabilized sufficiently to be able to baby sit for another lady's child for a couple of years until the child got old enough to go to school. When she lost that job, she became interested in getting employment at a department store where she had once worked, early in her marriage, and where she had been a very successful clerk.

Then an unfortunate event occurred; the outpatient clinic's psychiatric staff was changed and a new physician took over the service. Lacking psychiatric training and experience, he rather unilaterally took all the clinic patients off of their medications. In Mrs. D's case he told her she had done well for some time and could get along without any more medicine. Within four months from the time her prescription was stopped, Mrs. D. became increasingly disturbed, hallucinatory, and delusional. She attacked her husband and began her old pattern of harrassment of the neighbors. It was necessary to hospitalize her when the husband decided that she was dangerous to herself and others. It took the hospital staff a month to calm her down. In the interim, she upset other patients on the ward by slapping them without apparent provocation and verbally hurling obscenities at them; she stated that she hated the hospital and the patients. But, once stabilized on medication, her controls improved and she was discharged.

Neither Mr. nor Mrs. D. associated the patient's psychotic episode with the discontinuance of her medications. Mr. D. said he was very disappointed in her relapse because he thought she had gotten better; Mrs. D. said she got upset about the horrible people (blacks) that were moving into the neighborhood and were raping people, that this was why she couldn't sleep and had to go to the hospital. If we had not searched the clinic records, there would have been no way to note the direct relationship between this patient's follow-up failure and the fact that her medications had been discontinued.

We have used this case because it unfortunately represents but one of many others that show that continued medical maintenance is an absolute necessity and at times is the only vehicle available for helping chronic schizophrenics to make a community adjustment. This is particularly true with patients such as Mrs. D. who have lengthy histories of hospitalization and whose daily lives and families have few positive resources to offer them.

Home Care Placebo Failure: Follow-up Success

The case of Wayne C. provides us with some insights into the extent to which patient behavior can change depending upon the base pathology, the family configuration, and the availability of appropriate psychiatric attention. Mr. C. was referred to ITC by the state mental hospital where he had been admitted only three days previously. His hospitalization was precipitated by his excessive drinking, a job loss, and his increasing suspiciousness, hostility, and withdrawal from reality. He ultimately became disturbed to the degree that he threatened to kill himself as well as his wife and children. He was diagnosed as having a schizophrenic reaction, paranoid type. His symptoms had not abated by the time of his referral to ITC, but his wife was eager to have him home and was willing to cooperate with the home care project.

Mr. C. was a 39-year-old married, white male with four children ranging in age from two to 15 years; at the time of ITC intake his wife was pregnant with their fifth child. Mr. C. had been hospitalized once before, at the age of 25, but he had functioned in the intervening years without overt psychiatric difficulty. He worked as a bricklayer and when he was working the family seemed at best to experience few financial problems.

His wife was a sympathetic and fairly attractive woman, two years younger than he. She was puzzled and distressed by the current illness and was willing to cooperate with ITC in any way possible to help her husband. Unbeknown to the staff, Mr. C.'s medications were placebos and they proved to be totally ineffective in preventing his slow and complete schizophrenic withdrawal.

Mr. C. was too ill to work and in short order the family was having severe financial difficulties. They had to move from their rental home in the city to a cheaper rural facility, which had no central heat or running water. Mr. C. was too disturbed to be able to do anything around the home to help his wife; he would either sit in a chair and stare into space mumbling incoherently, or he would pace about the rooms in an agitated manner. He would not permit his wife to leave his side, refusing to let her out of the house to do the necessary chores; he was fearful that something would happen to one of them.

Mrs. C. was, by this time, five months pregnant and it was necessary for her to chop wood for their stove and to haul water from the well. The strain on her health soon became obvious; she was pale, thin, tense, tired, and highly anxious about their situation. ITC, in an effort to help, assisted them to apply for Social Security disability checks, but the application's approval took four months and by the time their first payment arrived the family situation had deteriorated beyond reprieve.

Mr. C. had grown progressively worse; he did not sleep, nor did he eat; he was totally noncommunicative with the ITC nurse. The nurse, with decreasing assurance, tried to maintain a positive outlook, but the situation did not improve and it became apparent that Mrs. C. would soon end up as a second patient if something were not done about her husband and the hardships of their living situation. After repeated consultations with the staff psychiatrist and a futile attempt to utilize outpatient shock treatment, which could not be arranged due to transportation problems, the decision was reached to return Mr. C. to the hospital for intensive attention. The patient, after six months on placebo home care, had obviously failed and he had to be hospitalized.

Mr. C. responded to hospital care and the medications. He was released from the hospital after two months of inpatient care. He was thereafter referred to the hospital's outpatient clinic, which he attended fairly regularly for a number of years. At the time of the follow-up, five years later, the nurse reported that Mr. C. was obviously a different person from what he had been during ITC; he had gained weight, was talkative, happy, and showed few signs of emotional difficulty. Mrs. C., likewise, was different; she was responsive, free from worry, and reported that the family was doing well. Mr. C. was working regularly and the family moved from town to town in their trailer following construction jobs. They had also bought two acres of land in a town outside of Louisville and planned to build a home and settle there as soon as Mr. C.'s jobs would permit this. Mr. C. earned approximately $300 per week, as a bricklayer, liked his work, and the family had enough money to take a vacation each year. The children were happy, well fed, and were doing well in school. Mr. C. felt that his earlier problems had been due to excessive drinking and he said he no longer drank, therefore neither he nor his wife expected future problems. In short, the follow-up visit seemed to indicate a positive prognosis for the patient and his family.

We should at this time like to review the nature of the outpatient attention Mr. C. received over the follow-up years and also suggest why we are less assured about Mr. C.'s continued positive adjustment. In 1964, at the end of the ITC program, Mr. C. attended the clinic once every two months; the clinic records noted that he was decreasing his own medicines and this practice was approved by the clinic doctor; Mr. C. was also given permission by the social worker to drink in moderation. For the next year he attended the clinic once in every four months and was taking 5 milligrams of Stelazine once every other night. The year after, in January of 1966, he was discharged from the clinic by his doctor and was told that he could return whenever he wished to get medicine if he thought that he needed it. Within three months of his discharge the patient returned, asking to continue talking with the social worker and to get medication. He came thereafter once every other month until September of that year, when he ceased to attend. He was absent from the clinic for an entire year until September of 1967, when he came in to talk with the doctor; but at this time no medications were given, he was merely counseled on how to have his civil rights restored. No further clinic contact occurred until almost another year had passed.

In June of 1968, yet another year later, the patient came to the clinic and was seen by a new doctor and a new social worker. At this time Mr. C. was experiencing a recurrence of psychiatric difficulties; he was suspicious, said he was hearing voices; and he was unable to work. He was given a prescription for Stelazine, 5 milligrams, to be taken twice a day. That prescription lasted until September and Mr. C. did not return to the clinic for further medication. He was not seen again until the follow-up interview, which took place eight months later, in 1969—and at that time he appeared to be doing well.

Considering the extensity of Mr. C.'s disorder at ITC intake and his very positive response to maintenance doses of medication, further noting the recurrence of paranoid symptoms in 1968, it appears foolish for this patient to be advised that he need not continue supportive clinic contacts and maintenance doses of medicines. It would be more desirable if he attended the clinic at least twice yearly for a check up and for monitoring of his medical needs. Currently the patient, his family, as well as the clinic staff, appear well assured of Mr. C.'s good emotional health; but with our long-term research perspective we rest less assured and would advise against the termination of all outpatient attentions for patients with histories of serious schizophrenic symptoms. The risk of ceasing outpatient attention is too great when it involves any potential for a recurrence of symptoms and the concomitant crisis the disorder causes for patients and their families. We are therefore apprehensive about the prospects for Mr. C. given his withdrawal from all regular after-care support.

Conclusions

The preceding cases have been selected to provide the reader with an overview of the realities of existence confronting schizophrenics and their families. We have chosen to emphasize that the course taken by any one patient depends upon the following variables: (1) the intensity and extent of the patient's illness; (2) the degree of health or disorganization in the patient's family; (3) the availability of appropriate medication; and (4) the provision of adequate therapies such as social service help or supportive counseling, depending upon the needs of the patient and his family. We have emphasized the importance of continued medical supervision of patients, the value of knowledge of the family situation, the need to alleviate stress by the provision of social support to the family unit; and, last, the need for continuity in such care over prolonged periods. We have also included cases to show that there are exceptions to the rule: there are patients whose upsets are transitory and whose inherent tendencies toward a healthy adjustment suffice with minimal psychiatric intervention; and also to show that there are patients for whom none of our available psychiatric or social resources are of any avail. In sum, it behooves the psychiatric professionals to err more on the side of providing total and continuing services than to provide the currently too brief, or incomplete and discontinuous, services. With the use of a little more common sense and a socio-supportive approach, combined with an emphasis on continued medications, the treatment of schizophrenics could be vastly improved with a long-range decrease in the financial and social costs that we now all too frequently witness.

chapter seven

An Overview and Conclusions

The Original Study

In 1961 the original ITC home study[1] was initiated "to determine
(1) whether home care for schizophrenic patients was feasible,
(2) whether drug therapy was effective in preventing their hospitalization, and (3) whether home care was, in fact, a better or poorer
method of treatment that hospitalization."[2] To carry out this research
program a facility known as the Institute Treatment Center opened,
near downtown Louisville.

Two and one-half years after its inception the ITC study terminated; home drug treatment had proven to be feasible with schizophrenics. "Over 77 percent of the drug home care patients but only
some 34 percent of the placebo cases remained in the community
throughout their participation in the project."[3] Although home care
assisted a third of the placebo patients to stay at home without drugs,
their failure rate was significantly higher than the drug care patients.

1. The major portion of the information in this concluding chapter as well
as parts of Chapter 1 appeared in the *American Journal of Orthopsychiatry* 1,
no. 3 (April 1972) article, "The Prevention of Hospitalization in Schizophrenia:
Five Years After an Experimental Program," by Ann E. Davis, Simon Dinitz, and
Benjamin Pasamanick. Copyright, 1972, the American Orthopsychiatric Association, Inc. Reproduced by permission.

2. Pasamanick, Scarpitti, and Dinitz, *Schizophrenics in the Community*, p.
33.

3. Ibid., p. 250.

In answer to the question of whether patients fared better under home care or in routine hospital care, the drug home care group held the advantage. "Even after initial hospitalization averaging 83 days and the presumable remission of the grosser symptoms, the hospital controls failed more often at the termination of treatment than did the home care patients."[4] In terms of hospitalization time saved as well as on community performance home care drug patients did better. "Patients improved in mental status, psychological test performance, domestic functioning, and social participation. These gains were considerable and frequently statistically significant. In all of the many specific measures, home care patients were functioning as well or better than the hospital control cases."[5]

The experiment proved successful in demonstrating that florid episodes could be controlled at home and chronic schizophrenic patients could be saved expensive days of hospital care, but it had to be stressed that patients continued to be marginal in routine daily task performances. The researchers said, "On the instrumental role performance level, some of the home care patients as well some of the controls were still exhibiting low quality performance."[6]

The Follow-up (1964-1969)

Plans for a follow-up study were enhanced by a number of fortuitous circumstances. The original project social worker was available for and interested in an evaluation of the original program. Four of the original five project nurses had continued their employment with the Kentucky Department of Mental Health as community care nurses and had maintained contact with many of the patients. The psychiatrist, psychologist, and numerous other state hospital personnel were still in the community available to assist in a restudy as needed.

The follow-up was designed to test several hypotheses. The most important were these:

1.   There would be no significant difference between the home care and hospital control groups in rates of rehospitalization and in days of hospitalization in the post-ITC home care period (1964-1969).

4.   Ibid.
5.   Ibid., p. 251.
6.   Ibid.

The follow-up study sought to determine if ITC home care had any lasting effects; whether, in fact, the home care drug patients continued to hold a treatment advantage over the other two groups years after the ITC study ended.

2. There would be no significant difference between the home care and the control groups in terms of their levels of performance on vocational, social, domestic, marital, and psychological variables by the time of the five-year follow-up in 1969. The expectation was that the study groups would become indistinguishable from each other five years after the experimental ITC study.

3. There would be no improvement, over time, in the patients' performances on any of the major variables. The anticipation was that schizophrenia as a chronic disorder would result in reduced task performance over time.

Over 90 percent of the original sample subjects were located and studied. Among the basic instruments used for data collection were: (1) a formal interview schedule with the patient's SO (significant other); (2) an informal interview with the patient; (3) a psychiatric-rating scale completed by the SO; (4) a completely formalized search of all state and private hospital records to identify all patients hospitalized since the end of the ITC study; and (5) a complete formal search of all clinic records to document treatment received over the follow-up period. Given the personal knowledge of patients held by the ITC nurses, who were the interviewers, and by the researchers, data collection proceeded with minimal complications.

Study Results at Follow-up in 1969

Hospitalization Experiences

The first question the follow-up dealt with was: had the impact of ITC home care, which resulted in superior outcomes for the home care drug group, persisted after the project terminated? Analysis of follow-up data showed, as hypothesized, that there were no statistically significant differences among the groups (drug, placebo, and hospital control) on either days spent in the hospital, on the number of rehospitalizations, or on percentages of each group that were hospitalized. The drug group had averaged 125 days in the hospital in the post-ITC years, the placebo group 221, and the controls 136. Sixty-one percent of the drug patients were hospitalized over the follow-up, as were 57 percent of the placebo patients, and 61 percent of the controls. None of these differences were significant statistically. There were also no statistically significant differences among the groups on the extent of clinic care received during the follow-up. In short, once the unique home care experiment had terminated and patients were subjected to routine state care for mental patients, the patients' mental statuses and adjustments became similar. The ITC care was effective, therefore, only while it was an ongoing program. This fact demonstrated the necessity for continued after-care for this chronic mental disorder, and the fact that the concept of cure should be treated with caution for schizophrenics.

ITC Treatment Effects over Time

ITC home care drug patients had a marked psychiatric adjustment advantage at the beginning of the follow-up (the end of ITC); this superiority was maintained for a brief time after ITC home care terminated; the drug patients remained out of the hospital longer than the placebo patients. The placebo patients, in poorer psychiatric condition at the end of ITC (due to drug deprivation), had to be hospitalized soon after the experiment ended. Placebo patients also averaged longer periods of inhospital care over the post-ITC period.

After ITC home care terminated, home care drug patients were better for a short while and placebo patients were worse for that same short while; the control patients remained in an intermediate position. However, by the time of the five-year follow-up no differences in hospital or clinic care treatment experiences could be found among the study groups; similar post-ITC care had equalized their demand for psychiatric attentions.

Also, at the time of follow-up in 1969 there were no significant differences among the groups on their psychiatric status scores on the Lorr scale. The overwhelming evidence, based on these scale scores, was in support of the hypothesis that the psychological condition of the patients in the drug, placebo, and control groups was not significantly different by the time of the follow-up study. These results were congruent with findings on the hospital and clinic treatment experiences.

Problem Behaviors

Problems that patients exhibited at home were closely related to their mental condition. The social problems checklist that measured the degree of patients' problem behavior at home supported previous findings. It showed that the groups did not differ significantly from each other by the end of the follow-up.

Rank-ordering of problems revealed that the most frequently named items were intrapsychic in nature. For example, SOs in all groups stated that they worried a great deal about the patient. Worries were frequently caused by the bizarre speech, ideas, and actions expressed by patients. SOs were alarmed about the welfare of the patient, their households were disrupted, and the coping abilities of family members were frequently exhausted. The end result was that psychiatric attentions were sought for, and subsequent relief sought from, the disordered patient by the family.

Vocational and Domestic Performance

Data on domestic and vocational performance showed that the study groups did not differ from each other on economic or work related variables. Most patients had histories of unemployment or unemployability; those who had worked usually had exceedingly poor work-performance records. Only 27 percent of the drug group patients, 26 percent of the placebo patients, and 27 percent of the controls had any occupation, even that of common laborer. Many patients were among those considered too disabled to work either mentally or physically; this was true of 28 percent of the drug group, 49 percent of the placebos, and 32 percent of the control patients.

Almost half of the patients were the primary financial support of the family; their scource of income was generally common labor or a welfare grant. Placebo patients were more likely to be welfare recipients; they had qualified on the basis of mental disability. This situation was explained by their disproportionate needs for financial support dating back to the original ITC study when, because of drug deprivation during that period, they were more noticeably disabled. Their dependency upon welfare grants never changed in the ensuing years.

On domestic performance variables there were no significant differences on mean total scores. Task performance and instrumental measures were not as revealing of the post-ITC adjustment of the patients as were hospitalization and clinic treatment measures. Performance variables were considered less of a measure of the patients' mental status than were the hard-data treatment variables such as the number of hospital days or clinic days under care. Many social factors such as age, family expectations, and role demands impinged upon and altered patients' performances making these variables less clearly related to patients' psychiatric statuses. Nonetheless, a majority of the performance variables offered support for the thesis that no significant difference among the groups would be found five years after termination of the ITC home care program.

Longitudinal Evaluation Results
Focusing upon Differential Treatment Impacts

Psychiatric Status over Time (1962–1969)
(ITC Home Care Inclusive of the Follow-up Time Period)

The placebo patients, as measured by the Lorr scale, were the sickest group at the end of ITC. This was obviously due to their drug deprivation during ITC. Once the project terminated the patients given placebos were referred for psychiatric attention and received drugs from both the hospitals and the clinics. By the time of the follow-up the placebo group had markedly improved in psychiatric symptom scores compared with the home care drug patients. Also, once ITC home care ended the drug patients began to receive routine state outpatient clinic and hospital attention, their psychiatric status deteriorated somewhat given the withdrawal of special ITC home care socio-supportive attention; but their condition never deteriorated to the point at which it was at ITC intake. The placebo group had improved only minimally during ITC: it will be recalled that over 77 percent of the drug home care patients but only 34 percent of the placebo patients remained continuously at home during the ITC home care project. But by the time of the follow-up the drug group's better experience was gone and the percentage of their lifetimes spent in the hospital did not differ from other groups. The effects of ITC home care had disappeared leaving the three groups comparable.

Longitudinal Community Performance and Adjustment (1962–1969)

Long-term community performance and adjustment results were similar to those received on the Lorr psychiatric scale and on the problems checklist. The worst scores were recorded at ITC intake when all patients were experiencing psychotic episodes. All groups had shown a reduction in problems behavior by the end of ITC care. Such reductions were far more dramatic for the home care drug patients than for the placebo group; but by the time of the follow-up, in 1969, the drug group's functioning had deteriorated thereby testifying to the superiority of ITC home drug care, as evidenced during the experimental project, over routine state clinic care for assisting patients' psychological adjustments. Conversely the placebo patients scores improved in the post-ITC period after receipt of state care, because attention with drugs was superior to ITC home care without them.

Thus, the performance of the home care drug group supported the hypothesis positing increased impairments after ITC ended, but the experience of the placebo group did not. The placebo group improved for they were treated with drugs following the termination of home care, again supporting the fact that drugs are essential for care of schizophrenics.

Domestic Performance (1962–1969)

Patients in all groups deteriorated on task performance over time. The instrumental performance scores at follow-up were worse than scores at either ITC intake or at the termination of ITC home care. Thus, post-ITC drug care did not save the placebo patients or others from increasingly poorer performances on routine task measures.

Task performance scores were not highly correlated with psychiatric treatment status. Reasons for this lay in the advancing age of patients that slowed adjustment capacities and task performance abilities. Also, as importantly, repeated negative labeling and a history of poor performance tended to lower both patients' and SOs' expectations and thence patients' performances. Some patients, after many emotional upsets and treatment, no longer tried to perform routine household and vocational tasks. Patients severed their marital and family ties more than they created new ones; thus these instabilities also acted to reduce the necessity, and expectations, for adequate task performance.

Social Participation (1962–1969)

On the social participation measure a majority, around 51 percent of the patients in each of the three groups, remained in status quo or lessened their activities once ITC home care ended. All groups showed poorer scores at follow-up than at ITC intake on friendship patterns and interpersonal abilities.

The specific task performance measures: vocational, domestic, and social participation indicated, with rare exception, that patients did not improve over time in their performance but rather their performances generally worsened. Considerable evidence was amassed showing the lack of impact of formal psychiatric care on patients' abilities to perform tasks and to participate in social activities. Therefore we concluded that task and performance measures were not as closely correlated to psychiatric adjustment as were direct measures of psychiatric status and measures of problematic home behavior.

Successes and Failures

Having demonstrated that the study groups did not differ significantly from each other at the end of the five-year follow-up, the analysis moved toward isolating the factors predictive of rehospitalization. The three original study groups, drug, placebo, and hospital control, were combined and then regrouped into two categories, successes and failures. Successes were defined as patients who avoided rehospitalization in the post-ITC home care period and failures as those who required hospitalization.

Failures could be differentiated in a statistically significant manner on only one of the demographic characteristics examined. They were less likely to be married at the end of the follow-up time than successes. There was also a tendency for patients with low social status, for women and for blacks, to predominate among the failures.

Psychiatric Factors

The Lorr psychiatric scale scores, as might have been expected, produced the most significant differentials between successes and failures. All scores including the total scale score, with one exception, showed that the failures were significantly psychiatrically sicker, that is, they had more severe symptoms than the successes over the follow-up period.

Almost as highly related to success and failure as the psychiatric inventory findings were the scores on the problems checklist. Over half of the individual problems checklist items, as well as the total score, showed the failures to be significantly behaviorally more problematic than the successes. Problems most frequently cited by SOs were those dealing with odd and bizarre behaviors, especially strange speech and ideation, as well as the resultant upsets this behavior caused SOs and the entire household.

Hospital Histories prior to ITC

It was anticipated that failures would have significantly more lengthy hospital histories than the successes. This expectation was supported only in part. Poorer histories were reported for the time period covering the ITC home care years for the failures, whereas prior to ITC home care no consistently significant differences could be found. Pre-ITC data on hospitalizations may have been less accurate in that it depended solely upon the abilities of the SOs to recall previous hospitalizations. The general conclusion was that over the years from 1962 to 1969 pre-ITC experiences were moderately predictive of success and failure and ITC hospital experiences were highly predictive of hospitalization experiences during the follow-up period.

Clinic Data

Clinic attendance reports over the post-ITC home care period showed that failures were significantly more likely to have *ever* attended a clinic. In contrast (much to our surprise) the amount of care utilized, that is, the total number of contacts and the mean percentage of nonhospitalized time spent under clinic care, failed to distinguish significantly between the successes and the failures.

As attenders both groups made use of clinic services in near equal degrees, but the major finding concerning clinics was that the two groups differed in the way they utilized the clinic and in the way clinic personnel responded to them. Higher percentages of successes attended clinic regularly, and greater numbers of these patients and their families were cooperative with clinic personnel. Most important, significantly more successes were taking their medication regularly, as prescribed, and we felt this to be a critical variable in explaining rehospitalizations. The clinic's response to the cooperation of the successful patients was a program tailored to their needs; the interaction between successes and clinical personnel was positive.

Failures and their families, in contrast, were significantly less cooperative with the outpatient clinic's staff. The families of failures were beset by more problems than the families of successes; there was also more psychopathology among their family members. Significantly, only 2 percent of the failures were taking the prescribed stabilized dosage of medicine, regularly, prior to their hospitalization. Clinic care evidently was not as well suited to the needs of the failures as to the successes. Failures were largely noncooperative and difficult to manage; they made sporadic and poor use of clinic facilities. Staffs of the clinics, in turn, responded rather unenthusiastically toward them. We concluded that clinics were in fact failing to prevent rehospitalizations, being ill equipped to sufficiently pursue the noncooperative patient and problem families. Another serious deficit was the insufficient attention being paid to the continuance of medications for patients who attended clinic and the necessity of educating families and patients to this need for regular use of medication.

Precipitants of Hospitalization

Intrapsychic (endogenous) problems proved to be the most important single item differentiating failure from success in rehospitalizations over the post-ITC period. Surprisingly, interpersonal problems were comparatively more prevalent among successes and were not closely related to rehospitalization; also economic stresses and other external social stresses—such as death, job losses, and physical problems—did not coincide with periods immediately preceding rehospitalization. In essence psychotic episodes were not triggered by any immediate, apparent, or external (to the patient) difficulty. Psychotic episodes, despite the psychiatric literature, were seemingly attributable to internal, intrapsychic problems with no visible external precipitants. This is an important finding and is in accord with other studies that lend support to a possible physical basis for schizophrenic disorder.

Economic, Domestic, and Social Variables
in Rehospitalization

No significant differences were found between the successes and failures on domestic task performance nor on social participation scores. There was some evidence, however, that successful patients tended to be less dependent upon siblings, children, or parents. They were more likely to be employed, whether they were men or women patients, and they were slightly more competent (not statistically significant) in their task performances. Successes had fewer people available to substitute for them on their tasks when they failed to personally perform them. Recalling that successes were more likely to be married, note was taken of the interactive effects of better performance, preservation of the marital situation, and higher expectations that may have resulted in the modestly better performance of the successes. Failures, conversely, were more often unmarried, more dependent, less often working outside the home, and had more role replacements available to help them. The reverse of the expectation-performance cycle was operative for such patients; low performance fostered low expectations, which in turn reinforced the low expectations among failures and their families.

Note was taken throughout the study that failures were less likely to be, or remain, married. Clinic and hospital records as well as interview data suggested that they related more pathologically to the opposite sex, broke ties often with members of both sexes (probably because of psychopathology) and, after severing such ties, were four times more likely to live alone than the successes.

Comments on the Nature of Schizophrenia

The data clearly pointed to schizophrenic upsets and episodes as occurring without noticeable external precipitants. When a patient became upset his ideation, perception, memory, speech, and actions became bizarre; actions became unpredictable, This, in turn, alarmed and threatened families arousing fears concerning the well-being of the patients as well as that of the SOs and other members of the household. The data indicated that this configuration of alarm, threat, and familial disorder led to the hospitalization of the patient.

The Treatment of Schizophrenics

The course of the disorder from the time of the first treatment contact may be altered depending upon the kind of treatment given and the extensiveness and intensity of the disease process. There is evidence in this study to show that patients with the more severe disorders tended to have the most difficulty throughout the many years of our research involvement with them even though the frequency of episodes and hospitalizations could be controlled by medication, and by the addition of home care socio-supportive attention. In essence, the severity of the disorder was, as a physiological base, fairly consistent over time.

Treatment intervention, if it included the psychoactive drugs (as during ITC home care, or clinic care with drugs), generally improved the patients' mental statuses and sometimes their task performances, as well as prevented rehospitalization. Whenever the drugs were withdrawn or the patients ceased taking medication they were likely to experience other episodes and rehospitalizations despite other socio-supportive attentions as witnessed in the home care placebo group and in the high numbers of patients rehospitalized who were not taking medication over the follow-up period. The data in the initial ITC study and in this follow-up study demonstrated that drug care had to be maintained to minimize or prevent recurrent psychotic episodes. If the drug care is supplemented by family oriented socio-supportive care better adjustments are evidenced.

Care, as given by most of the outpatient clinics and by the state hospitals' aftercare clinics, fails to prevent rehospitalizations because such facilities rely upon patient initiative for attendance and upon the patients' and families' cooperation and trust. Most importantly, the clinics depend upon the patients' willingness to be personally responsible for taking prescribed medications. Clinic personnel frequently assume that discontinuation or decrease in drug dosage is proper and wise medical practice for the convalescing mental patient. When treating schizophrenics these are erroneous assumptions; schizophrenia as depicted by our data is a chronic disorder, and the needs for medication do not, in fact, diminish even when patients appear to be doing well.

Psychiatric clinics, like other medical facilities, operate on the assumption that patients are rational, responsible, and interested in improving their health status. This model simply does not apply for most disordered, disoriented, or psychotic patients. It may, however, apply to the types of patients seen in the traditional outpatient psychiatric clinics—the neurotic, the character disordered, and the psychophysiologic problem cases who are largely middle class, well educated, and more likely to be self-directing and oriented to personal problem-solving.

Since clinics are being called upon to play a major role in providing community care for schizophrenic patients, the voluntaristic model and its assumptions should be replaced by an aggressive delivery system designed to deal with chronic, lower-class, marginal patients, like the psychotics in this study and those who comprise the bulk of state hospital populations.

ITC home care proved the most effective format for two basic reasons: first, drugs were taken to the homes by a nurse who urged the families to supervise the patients' taking of prescribed medications. No patient was taken off medication because he was considered cured or sufficiently improved to be without drugs. Second, nurses went out regularly to the patients' homes. They did not allow the patients to assume the initiative for the treatment contact, instead they reached out to give the necessary care. In the homes nurses interacted with the families and gave them much needed emotional support and practical problem-solving guidance. (This fact was not fully appreciated during the analysis of our initial study data.) ITC, through social work services, also provided social referrals to help with health problems, job training, and financial aid, as well as with other social needs.

Taking the program to the family was needed to stabilize the lower-class multi-problem families in which these schizophrenics were frequently a serious disorganizing factor. When left without supportive attention families with sick patients, whose episodes were recurrent, were likely to abandon the patients and, as our data clearly show, leave them living alone or in the homes of other than primary family members. To reiterate, the most important finding of the study was: that chronic schizophrenics, in order to remain successfully in the community, must have continuous supervision and medication. They and their families must receive social services and emotional support to alleviate the all-too-familiar patterns of personal and family disorganization.

We have been unable to claim that daily routine task performance and social behavior will improve over time by drug home care. The data strongly suggest that task performance deteriorates over time whether the patients receive outpatient, or inpatient, care. The ITC home care project was successful in decreasing (somewhat) the numbers of patients who needed assistance in performing their instrumental tasks. Such improvement took place even among the placebo patients who were not receiving medication. This led us to consider that entrustment with responsibility plus the expectation for performance may be necessary for the continued performance of domestic tasks. Following ITC home care, however, with the resumption of routine state outpatient or state hospital care (such care too often excludes active concern with patients' task activities) the vast majority of the patients tended to deteriorate markedly in their daily functioning. An assumption that needs to be tested is: If we had available intensive "coordinated," and variable facilities, including day hospitals, sheltered workshops, hostels, inpatient and outpatient and home care, would we be able to improve task functioning?

Similarly the employment and employability of the patients in the post-ITC home care period also deteriorated markedly regardless of the nature of the state's post-ITC treatment intervention. Data on social participation and in particular on patients' patterns of marital and interpersonal relationships were congruent with other community adjustment findings indicating increasing debilitation in the post-ITC home care period. The evidence is that routine community or hospital psychiatric care will not prevent, or significantly retard, the deterioration of patients' performances and adjustments on domestic, vocational, social, and marital variables.

Medications are able to prevent or at least delay psychotic episodes. It remains for psychiatric or social care to prevent the social and task performance deterioration of patients. Rather than being integrated into community life most ex-mental patients withdraw, become increasingly home bound, and essentially nonactive; they are nonparticipants in the society of today. The unique contribution of this research may be in calling attention to the absolute necessity of continued surveillance and community treatment of former hospital patients.

Obviously, whether as responsible treatment persons or simply as citizens, we cannot help but respond to the necessity of assisting patients to become functioning members of society. Now that the drug revolution has managed to minimize the overt disruptions and acute evidences of psychoses, the even larger task of activating and reintegrating patients into the community waits to be faced. Without such an effort we have merely transferred schizophrenic patients to the custodial back "wards" of their homes and communities.

appendix A

Letters and Release of Information Form

COMMONWEALTH OF KENTUCKY

DEPARTMENT OF MENTAL HEALTH

February 27, 1969

Dear

     Our department is contacting a number of people who at one time, received services from the psychiatric treatment facilities in Jefferson county. Our interest is in learning how you and others are getting along now and about the kinds of programs and services that were a help to you in the past.

     The information that we gain will help us in our efforts to learn more about what kinds of care or services are useful and how we will be able to give more effective help to more individuals.

     In the near future you will either be visited by a representative from our department or you will receive a questionnaire in the mail. We appreciate all the help and cooperation you can give us.

                    Sincerely,

                    Ann E. Davis
                    Consultant, Department
                    of Mental Health
                    c/o Elizabeth Baker RN
                    Central Hospital
                    (Outpatient Clinic)
                    Anchorage, Kentucky

COMMONWEALTH OF KENTUCKY

DEPARTMENT OF MENTAL HEALTH

Dear

      At one time   was cared for by the Institute Treatment Center in Louisville. We have been locating all the clients, and their families, that were once under our care, to see how they have gotten along since the end of our program in 1964.

      As part of the study we have been interviewing all of the people that live near Louisville. Since you have moved we cannot talk to you personally so we are asking you to fill out the enclosed form, as well as you can, and to return it to us. Your efforts will be very much appreciated since this is one of the only ways that we can learn more about people and how they are or are not helped by our programs.

      Your answers are important and we appreciate the time you give this. There is a post paid envelope enclosed, please send the questionnaire back in it.

                                Most Sincerely,

                                Ann E. Davis
                                Consultant, Kentucky
                                Dept. of Mental Health

DATE: _____

THIS WILL AUTHORIZE Louisville General Hospital, The Kentucky
State Hospitals; other hospitals, clinics, and doctors

TO FURNISH INFORMATION OF A MEDICAL, SURGICAL AND SOCIAL NATURE
FROM THE RECORDS OF:_____

TO The Study c/o The Kentucky Department of Mental Health

_____
Signature of Respondent

_____
Signature of relative or SO

_____

appendix B

SO and Patient Interview Schedules
(Including the Lorr Scale)

SO INTERVIEW SCHEDULE

Pt's Name _____ Case Number_____

Pt's Group Assignment_____ Medication Status_____

For this follow up the patient is: (check appropriate status)

   a) Located _____ Deceased _____ Moved from Locale _____ D/K_____

   b) Interviewed_____ Refused Interview_____ Other _____

For this follow up the SO is: (Check appropriate status)

   a) Same as last ITC SO _____ New SO_____

   b) Interviewed _____ Refused Interview _____ Other _____

Pt's Address (include hospital) _____

_____ Phone _____

SO's Address (If same as the patient's state same) _____

_____

Name of Interviewer _____ Date _____

VOCATIONAL INFORMATION

1. Pt's current occupation_____

2. Since ITC (or the summer of 1964) has the pt had any type of
   special job training exclusive of the military? (Specify the
   type and length of time of training) no_____ yes _____ _____

   _____

   _____

3. Since ITC (or the summer of 1964) has the pt had any further
   education? (Specify the amount and type of education) no _____
   yes_____ _____

4. Since ITC, has the pt served in the armed services? (Describe the
   type of experience and the type of discharge) no _____ yes _____

   _____

   Length of time in the service?_____

5. Pt's work history since ITC (or the summer of 1964)

Job Held (Type of Work)	Hours Per Week	Dates From	To	Salary	Reason Terminated
_____	_____	_____	_____	_____	_____
_____	_____	_____	_____	_____	_____
_____	_____	_____	_____	_____	_____
_____	_____	_____	_____	_____	_____
_____	_____	_____	_____	_____	_____
_____	_____	_____	_____	_____	_____

6. What is the pt's current source of support? (all sources; note amount of each)

_____ Amount per wk? _____

_____

_____

7. If the pt is not working is he looking for a job? no____ yes ___
   If yes: for what kind of a job?_____

_____

8. What is the pt's biggest problem in terms of work?_____

_____

_____

9. When the pt is working, how good is his attendance on the job?
   a) When he is absent it is with good reason _____
   b) He is out from time to time without good reason _____
   c) He is frequently absent without cause _____
   d) He is absent most of the time _____

10. In general how difficult has it been for the pt to work?
    a) Not difficult at all _____
    b) Some difficulty _____
    c) Very difficult _____
    If difficulty: Explain _____

_____

11. If the pt isn't working: Why isn't he working?
    a) Too sick (physical) _____
    b) Too sick (mental) _____
    c) He doesn't want to work _____ Why? _____

    _____
    d) He can't get hired _____ Why? _____

    _____
    e) Housewife isn't expected to work _____
    f) Other _____

SOCIO-ECONOMIC STATUS

12. Who is the main breadwinner in the pt's household? (check one)
    Pt_____ Pt's father_____ Pt's mother_____ Pt's husband _____
    Pt's wife_____ Other (give relationship to Pt) _____

13. Is this the same breadwinner as during ITC? Yes_____ No_____
    If no: Who was the breadwinner at that time? _____

    If the breadwinner is other than the pt; what is the breadwinner's
    occupation?_____

15. If the breadwinner is other than the pt, is he:
    a) self employed _____
    b) regular job with regular income (full time) _____
    c) regular job with regular income (part time) _____
    d) sporadically employed _____
    e) a farmer _____ tenant _____ size farm _____
    f) retired _____ source of income _____
    g) welfare recipient _____
    h) pension recipient _____ what kind _____

16. What is the breadwinner's income? (only if other than the pt)
    (Note if weekly, monthly, or yearly and include all sources)

    _____

17. If other than the pt, what is the breadwinner's level of education?
    _____

18. What is the total annual income in the pt's household?
    (Approximate and include all sources such as all individuals
    working in the household, rental property, etc.) _____

    _____

HOUSEHOLD COMPOSITION

19. Household changed since ITC: (If the pt has moved, please fill in
    the following, listing moves from the time of ITC to the
    present)

	Residence Type	Dates		Lived with Whom
		From	To	
1964	_____	_____	_____	_____
1965	_____	_____	_____	_____
1966	_____	_____	_____	_____
1967	_____	_____	_____	_____
1968	_____	_____	_____	_____
Present	_____	_____	_____	_____

Reason for Move to this Home

1964	_____
1965	_____
1966	_____
1967	_____
1968	_____
Present	_____

20. Of all the households the pt has lived in, in which one did
    a) he get along the best?_____
    b) Who was he living with?_____
    c) Why did he get along well here?_____
    _____
    d) When was this? _____

21. Has the pt's marital status changed since ITC? (include common
    law marriages) no_____ yes_____

Person lived with	From	To	State of legality	Reason Separated
_____	___	___	_____	_____
_____	___	___	_____	_____
_____	___	___	_____	_____

22. Explore and describe briefly the way the pt has gotten along
    with the opposite sex. (The frequency of dates, seriousness of
    relationships, interest in other sex, and his difficulties
    with heterosexual relationships.)

23. If the interviewer has information volunteered by the SO, note the pt's involvement in homosexual relationships. _____
_____
_____

24. How does the SO feel that the pt would be best off?
Single_____ Married_____ With Children_____ Without Children_____

25. List the persons living in the pt's current household:

Relation to Pt.	Age	Relation to Pt.	Age
_____	_____	_____	_____
_____	_____	_____	_____
_____	_____	_____	_____
_____	_____	_____	_____
_____	_____	_____	_____

26. What is the pt's relationship with the following people:
(Place an asterisk by the name of the person with whom the pt has the most conflict. Circle the person on whom the pt is most dependent.)

Relationship Rating (Check one)

	Excellent	Good	Fair	Poor
Mother	_____	_____	_____	_____
Father	_____	_____	_____	_____
Brother(s)	_____	_____	_____	_____
Sister(s)	_____	_____	_____	_____
Adult children	_____	_____	_____	_____
Spouse	_____	_____	_____	_____
Mother In Law	_____	_____	_____	_____
Father In Law	_____	_____	_____	_____
Other In Law	_____	_____	_____	_____
Boss	_____	_____	_____	_____
Other	_____	_____	_____	_____

26. (Continued)

| | Frequency of Contact (Check one) | | |
	Frequent	Occasional	Rare
Mother	____	____	____
Father	____	____	____
Brother(s)	____	____	____
Sister(s)	____	____	____
Adult children	____	____	____
Spouse	____	____	____
Mother In Law	____	____	____
Father In Law	____	____	____
Others In Law	____	____	____
Boss	____	____	____
Other	____	____	____

27. With what person in the household does the pt have the most
    problems? Who?_____
    What is the problem ? _____
    _____
    _____
    _____

28. With what people (not living in the home with the pt) does the
    pt have the most problems? (i.e., other relatives)
    Who? _____   What is the problem? _____
    _____   _____
    _____   _____
    _____   _____

29. If not the SO: Ask for a brief description of the following
    people. What kind of person is the. . .
    a) Pt's father_____
    _____
    b) Pt's mother_____
    _____
    c) Pt's spouse_____
    _____

30. Has any member of the family (relatives excluding the pt) had emotional problems? no____ yes____ (include ex-spouses)

Relation to pt	Date of problem	Duration	Nature of the problem
_____	_____	_____	_____
_____	_____	_____	_____
_____	_____	_____	_____
_____	_____	_____	_____
_____	_____	_____	_____

31. Has the pt had any children since ITC? no____ yes____

Sex	Current Age of Child	Where Child Lives Now
___	_____	_____
___	_____	_____
___	_____	_____

32. Do any of the pt's children have behavior problems such as bad behavior in the home, neighborhood, or school; delinquency or truancy? no____ yes____

Age of child	Sex	Nature of the Problem
_____	__	_____
_____	__	_____
_____	__	_____

33. Are any of the children behind in school? Or in special classes? no____ yes____

Age of child	Sex	Nature of the problem
_____	__	_____
_____	__	_____
_____	__	_____

34. Do any of the children have emotional problems; such as bed wetting, nightmares, nail biting, phobias, too much fighting, too shy, etc.? no____ yes____

Age of child	Sex	Nature of the problem
_____	__	_____
_____	__	_____
_____	__	_____

35. In general what would you say about the pt's ability to accept his responsibility as a parent?

    a) ____ An excellent parent: assumes full emotional and physical responsibility.

    b) ____ Good; occasional lapses, but responsibility is usually assumed.

    c) ____ Fair; some general failure to accept responsibility.

    d) ____ Poor; doesn't accept responsibility for children's rearing.

    e) ____ Nil; no significant emotional or physical contact between pt and children.

If the pt is rated either fair or poor, or nil, why does the SO feel the pt is this way? _____

Has the pt always been this way? _____

DOMESTIC PERFORMANCE

36. If the pt is a male, does he do any housework? no____ yes____ If yes, fill in the following for males and females.

37. Currently how much of the pt's time is spent in homemaking activities? If not full time indicate why not.

_____ Full time   If not full time reason why not:

_____ Over 75% of the time   _____

_____ Over 50% of the time   _____

_____ Very little time   _____

_____ None at all   _____

38. Who shares household duties with the pt? (List all helpers and the percentage of help given by each)

Individual Helping   Percent of Time

_____   _____

_____   _____

_____   _____

39. In the last month; (or if the pt is hospitalized, in the month
    prior to the hospitalization) did the pt. . . . .
    (Check chores the pt usually does even if she doesn't do the
    entire for the household, i.e., cleans her own room.)

Chore	Could Not Do	Needed Some Help (i.e., did poorly)	Did by Self (i.e., did OK)	Would Not	Did Not Have to
Housecleaning	____	____	____	____	____
Prepared meals	____	____	____	____	____
Laundry & cleaning	____	____	____	____	____
Grocery shopping	____	____	____	____	____
Other shopping	____	____	____	____	____
Budgeted & Paid Bills	____	____	____	____	____
Planned daily activities	____	____	____	____	____
Solved daily problems	____	____	____	____	____
Cared for children	____	____	____	____	____

40. How much of the housework do you feel that the pt is able to
    do? All_____ Most_____ Little_____ None_____
    If not all, why not?_____
    _____

41. In general would you say that the way the pt handles the
    housework is pretty much the way it was during ITC?
    Is it: Better_____ The same_____ or Worse_____. If worse,
    in what way?_____
    _____

42. Would you say that the pt is satisfied with being a homemaker?
    yes_____ no_____

43. If the pt had a choice between doing housework and having a job
    outside of the home, which would she choose?

    housework_____   a job_____   a combination_____

MENTAL TREATMENT HISTORY SINCE ITC (Since the summer of 1964)

IN HOSPITAL

44. Has the pt been in a mental hospital or psychiatric ward since
    ITC?   yes_____   no_____

Hospital Name	Type of Facility (VA, State or Private)	Dates From	To
a)_____	_____	_____	_____
b)_____	_____	_____	_____
c)_____	_____	_____	_____
d)_____	_____	_____	_____

45. For each hospitalization above give the reasons why the pt was
    hospitalized.
    a)_____
    b)_____
    c)_____
    d)_____

46. For each hospitalization above, who were the people involved in
    deciding that the pt should be hospitalized? (Note the person
    who made the final decision by placing an asterisk by his name.)
    a)_____
    b)_____
    c)_____
    d)_____

47. If and when the pt needs to be hospitalized, is it hard to get
    him there for care? no_____ yes_____   If yes: In what way?
    _____
    _____
    _____

OUT PATIENT CARE

48. Has the pt had any out patient treatment since ITC? no_____
    yes_____

Out Patient Agency	Type	From	To	Reason pt Went for Care
_____	_____	____	_____	_____
_____	_____	____	_____	_____
_____	_____	____	_____	_____

49. If and when the pt needs care is it hard to get him to a clinic or doctor? (Psychiatrist) yes_____ no_____
    If yes: what is the problem?_____

    _____

50. When the doctor prescribes medicine is it difficult to get the pt to take it? yes_____ no_____ If yes: why?_____

    _____

51. Does the pt have a family doctor? yes_____ no_____
    If yes: what is his name and address? _____

    _____

52. How does the pt get along with the family doctor? _____

    _____
    _____

53. How many visits has the pt made to a doctor in the last two years (not psychiatric visits) approximate._____

54. Since ITC list all the illnesses (physical) for which the pt was ill for more than one week, or which were serious enough that the pt visited a doctor.

Nature of Illness	Date	Duration	Dr. Consulted (yes or no)	If in Hospital (duration)
_____	___	_____	_____	_____
_____	___	_____	_____	_____
_____	___	_____	_____	_____
_____	___	_____	_____	_____

SOCIALIZATION

55. Does the pt drive? no_____ yes_____ What are the functions of his driving? (Check all that apply)
    work_____ household errands_____ pleasure_____ other_____

56. We are interested in the pt's friends. Would you say that:
    a) The pt has almost no friends and usually prefers to be by himself? _____
    b) The pt has a few friends, but has trouble getting along with them, or spends little time with them? _____
    c) The pt has friends and spends time with them, but does not always enjoy doing so? _____
    d) The pt has good friends and enjoys spending time with them? ___

57. How does the pt meet new people? (Briefly describe his
    general reaction, i.e., shy, friendly, talkative, etc.)
    _____
    _____

58. How are the pt's table manners? (Describe them briefly and
    include eating habits, i.e., appropriate and right amount of
    food behavior)_____
    _____

59. How is the pt's judgment with money? (Describe budgeting and
    buying habits)_____
    _____

60. How is the pt's dress (Briefly describe appropriateness)
    _____
    _____

PSYCHOLOGICAL STATUS

61. In the last four years, in terms of his psychological state or
    his nerves, how often has the pt been upset? Never_____
    Sometimes_____ A Lot_____

61(A) How many episodes in the last four years, has the pt had?_____

62. We are interested in knowing if, in the last month the patient
    has been a problem on the following things, and if, when he is
    nervous, he is a problem on the following things.

Problem	No	Some	A Lot
Patient is trouble at night:			
a) in the last month	_____	_____	_____
b) when nervous	_____	_____	_____
Pt's is a nursing problem bed-ridden, incontinent a feeding problem:			
a) in the last month	_____	_____	_____
b) when nervous	_____	_____	_____
Pt's safety is a source of worry (i.e., wandering, car driving):			
a) in the last month	_____	_____	_____
b) when nervous	_____	_____	_____

Problem	No	Some	A Lot
Pt causes worry about the safety of others:			
a) in the last month	____	____	____
b) when nervous	____	____	____
Pt has been difficult by being uncooperative:			
a) in the last month	____	____	____
b) when nervous	____	____	____
Pt is a strain by relying and depending on people too much:			
a) in the last month	____	____	____
b) when nervous	____	____	____
Pt's constant restlessness, or talking has been upsetting:			
a) in the last month	____	____	____
b) when nervous	____	____	____
Pt's frequent complaints about physical symptoms are worrisome:			
a) in the last month	____	____	____
b) when nervous	____	____	____
Pt is a problem because of rude, sexual or objectionable behavior:			
a) in the last month	____	____	____
b) when nervous	____	____	____
Pt is worrisome due to speaking or behaving oddly, or by having unusual or unreasonable ideas:			
a) in the last month	____	____	____
b) when nervous	____	____	____
Pt causes trouble with the neighbors:			
a) in the last month	____	____	____
b) when nervous	____	____	____

Problem	No	Some	A Lot
Pt upsets the household routine:			
a) in the last month	____	____	____
b) when nervous	____	____	____
Pt interferes with social or leisure activities:			
a) in the last month	____	____	____
b) when nervous	____	____	____
Someone in household has to stay away from work because of pt:			
a) in the last month	____	____	____
b) when nervous	____	____	____
Children have to stay away from school because of pt:			
a) in the last month	____	____	____
b) when nervous	____	____	____
The pt's behavior has caused SO much worry:			
a) in the last month	____	____	____
b) when nervous	____	____	____
Pt has been a physical strain on the SO:			
a) in the last month	____	____	____
b) when nervous	____	____	____
Pt requires a great deal of attention or companionship:			
a) in the last month	____	____	____
b) when nervous	____	____	____
Children in the family are ashamed because of the pt:			
a) in the last month	____	____	____
b) when nervous	____	____	____
The children in the family are afraid of the pt:			
a) in the last month	____	____	____
b) when nervous	____	____	____

Problem	No	Some	A Lot
The SO is ashamed of the pt:			
a) in the last month	____	____	____
b) when nervous	____	____	____
The SO is afraid of the pt:			
a) in the last month	____	____	____
b) when nervous	____	____	____

63. Does the pt often do the following things:

	No	Yes	Who does this bother?	What specific Things Are the Trouble?
a) Appear nervous?	____	____	_____	_____
b) Worry or complain a lot?	____	____	_____	_____
c) Argue with family members	____	____	_____	_____
d) Stay by himself a lot?	____	____	_____	_____
e) Talk senseless- ly, unhappily, or to himself a lot	____	____	_____	_____
f) Act strangely and do strange things?	____	____	_____	_____

64. Use of alcohol by pt:

Drinking Pattern	Current	Worst Drinking Period in last four years
a) Abstinent	_____	_____
b) Less than one drink per week (light drinking)	_____	_____
c) Two-three drinks per day (sometimes intoxicated)	_____	_____
d) Four-six drinks per day (regularly intoxicated, no trouble legally)	_____	_____
e) Occasionally in trouble socially or legally	_____	_____
f) Frequently in trouble outside the home (has lost jobs due to drinking)	_____	_____
g) Has had delirium tremens (include all cases irrespective of drinking pattern)	_____	_____
h) Alcoholic psychosis including D.T.'s, Korsakoff's hallucinosis, and deterioration.	_____	_____

64(B). Indicate the instances in which the SO would think about hospitalizing the pt in a mental hospital or psychiatric ward.

	Yes	Maybe	No
a) If he damaged or wrecked things	__	__	__
b) If he often appeared in a daze	__	__	__
c) If he exposed himself indecently	__	__	__
d) If he did not make sense when he talked	__	__	__
e) If he tried to hurt a neighbor or someone at work	__	__	__
f) If he said he heard voices	__	__	__
g) If he wouldn't do anything at home and just sat around	__	__	__

64(B) (Continued)

	Yes	Maybe	No
h) If he refused to eat	___	___	___
i) If he cried a great deal	___	___	___
j) If he was very frightened or worried all the time	___	___	___
k) If he refused to talk to anyone	___	___	___
l) If he laughed or was too happy and excited over nothing all the time	___	___	___
m) If he created scenes in front of neighbors and friends a great deal	___	___	___
n) If someone had to stay with him or watch him all the time	___	___	___
o) If he forgot things all the time	___	___	___
p) If he threatened to kill himself	___	___	___
q) If he was so sick he couldn't hold a job	___	___	___

FAMILY RELATIONS

65. We are interested in what things the family members do together, with the patient, and what things the pt does alone.

	With Others			Alone
	Often	Sometimes	Never	
a) Go shopping	___	___	___	___
b) Sit and talk to each other	___	___	___	___
c) Play cards, checkers, etc.	___	___	___	___
d) Go for walks	___	___	___	___
e) Go to movies	___	___	___	___
f) Watch TV	___	___	___	___
g) Go to church	___	___	___	___
h) Visit friends	___	___	___	___
i) Visit relatives	___	___	___	___
j) Go on picnics, trips, to beaches, or to parks	___	___	___	___
k) Sit down and eat	___	___	___	___

66. Have any of the following things happened during the past five
years in the patient's household (Include events happening in
other homes that the pt may have lived in during the last five
years)

	To Whom	When
a) An unusually serious money problem		
b) A serious school prob-lem		
c) A serious illness or accident		
d) A law suit		
e) A death		
f) Other (Indicate problem)		

67. If any of the following things have ever happened please tell us
when and describe what happened (Use N/A for no.)

Situation	When	What Happened?
a) Ever been frightened that the pt would hurt you physically?	a)	
b) Ever thought that the pt would hurt someone else?	b)	
c) That SO had to keep a watch on the pt more than is normal	c)	
d) SO has had to worry about his house or belongings around the pt	d)	
e) Has the pt ever gotten in the way of the SO doing his best that he could on his job?	e)	
f) Has the pt ever gotten in the way of the SO's raising his children just the way he wanted to?	f)	

67. (Continued)

Situation	When	What Happened?

g) Has the pt ever gotten
   in the way of SO's
   making the kind of
   friends he has wanted?   g) _____

h) Has the pt ever made
   the SO upset or
   embarrassed in front
   of others?   h) _____

i) Has the pt ever
   disappointed the
   SO very much?   i) _____

j) Has the pt ever gotten
   in the way of having
   the kind of home or
   family the SO wanted?   j) _____

68. If the SO were able to change the pt, what changes would he
    want most of all? _____

69. When the pt isn't living at home what is the biggest difference
    in the household? _____

70. When the pt is having problems do you think that:

		Yes	No
a) He is acting badly on purpose?		___	___
b) He could do better if he wanted to?		___	___
c) He is just contrary for no good reason?		___	___
d) He is spoiled and needs a firm hand?		___	___
e) He has always had moody spells and he is just that way?		___	___
f) He is mentally sick and needs treatment?		___	___
g) He is physically sick and needs treatment?		___	___
h) Nothing can be done about it since God has reasons for what He does?		___	___

71. What do you think the pt would change about you if he could?
    _____
    _____

72. Do you think that any of the pt's problems are your fault?
    no_____ yes_____ In what way? _____
    _____

FAMILY FLEXIBILITY

73. For the pt who is a wage earner: Is his income really impor-
    tant to the family? no_____ yes_____ If yes, when he can't
    earn a salary do you. . . . (check all that apply)

    _____ a) Go to the welfare department? What difficulties does
              this cause? _____
              _____

    _____ b) Does the spouse go to work, or does someone else in
              the family other than the spouse go to work?
              Who?_____
              If someone else goes to work what difficulties does
              this create? _____
              _____

    _____ c) Do relatives help you out? Who helps? _____
              And what difficulties does this cause? _____
              _____

74. For the pt who does housework: Is the pt's doing the housework
    really important to the family? no_____ yes_____ If yes: when
    the pt is too sick to do the housework, who does it?
    _____
    What difficulties does this cause? _____
    _____

75. For the pt with non-adult children. Is the pt's help really
    important in the supervision of the children? no_____ yes_____
    If yes: when the pt is too sick to supervise them who does?
    _____
    What difficulties does this cause?_____
    _____

76. In the last four years give the approximate dates and the length
    of time that it was necessary to get a replacement for the pt as:
                         When   Duration

    a) the wage earner   _____   _____
                           _____   _____

76. (Continued)

	When	Duration
b) Homemaker		
c) Child supervision		

77. Do you think in general that it would be better to demand more of the pt? _____ Or to demand less of the pt? _____

78. Do you think that the pt needs psychiatric treatment now? no_____ yes_____

79. What kind of treatment does the SO feel helps the pt?_____

   Is he getting this type of treatment now?_____

80. What does the SO feel is the pt's problem?_____

81. For the ITC home care pts. (Include all home care pts even failures and dropouts) What did you like about ITC?_____

82. For ITC home care pts (include failures and dropouts) What didn't you like about ITC?_____

83. If you had a chance to have the pt cared for on an ITC type of program would you want it available to him? no_____ yes_____

Interviewer Only: Please give your impressions about this SO . . . In terms of how he related to you during the interview; his attitudes toward the pt; and if you knew him during ITC any changes in him that you may have noticed since then.

It is my understanding that the information I give will be kept confidential and will be used by professionals for the purpose of bettering the care given to psychiatric patients.

SO signature_____

Date   _____

Patient's Name_____ Case Number _____

LORR RATING SCALE

Each question is preceded by the words, "Does the patient . . ." Before
each item you will see "YES NO"; if the person behaves the way
described you will circle YES; if the person does not behave that way
you will circle NO. Try to answer all questions!

Does the patient . . .

1. YES NO Speak in a very slow, unsure way?

2. YES NO Give answers that are completely unrelated to ques-
             tions asked or talk about things far off the topic
             being discussed?

3. YES NO Answer questions in a kind of double talk--grammar is
             very unusual or peculiar?

4. YES NO Tend to drift off the subject when in conversation?

5. YES NO Make hostile or nasty remarks about the people he
             knows?

6. YES NO Walk, sit, or stand in peculiar ways?

7. YES NO Laugh or cry for no reason.

8. YES NO Act as if he didn't care about getting well?

9. YES NO Speak in a very quick, hurried, or "pushed" manner?

10. YES NO Move around restlessly--very fidgety?

11. YES NO Act as if other people were unworthy or beneath him?

12. YES NO Act as if everything was wonderful and this is the
             best of all possible worlds?

13. YES NO Fix his face so that you can't tell what he is
             thinking or feeling?

14. YES NO Blame or condemn himself for all kinds of things that
             have happened either in the past or things going on
             right now?

15. YES NO Act in a conceited way--thinks he is superior or
             better than those around him?

16. YES NO   Seem to be very tired and worn out--even walking and moving seem to require special effort?

17. YES NO   Want to be the center of attraction--act in a "show-off way"?

18. YES NO   Act as if he had a chip on his shoulder?

19. YES NO   Have trouble remembering what has recently happened to him?

20. YES NO   Speak in a loud, intense tone of voice?

21. YES NO   Report that he is afraid or worried about such things as his illness, his family, or job?

22. YES NO   Although he does not usually stutter stammer, he has trouble like that when he talks.

23. YES NO   Seem to care about any of the things going on around him?

24. YES NO   Report that he is afraid or worried about things which are going to happen but he can't tell you what they are?

25. YES NO   Lose his temper quickly?

26. YES NO   Move around a lot when he is excited?

27. YES NO   Talk as if he felt inferior or useless no good to anyone?

28. YES NO   Blame other people for his troubles and problems?

29. YES NO   Always expect the worst to happen?

30. YES NO   Is he sloppy in his manners and appearance?

31. YES NO   Express guilt for having done wrong and say that he would like to make up for what he has done?

32. YES NO   Seem bitter because he feels other people have one him wrong?

33. YES NO   Speak in a low, weak voice or in whispers?

34. YES NO   Complain about anything and everything?

35. YES NO   Talk so much that it is hard to get a word in edgewise?

36. YES NO   Act in a very suspicious way towards those around him?

37. YES NO   Try to dominate or control the activities of those around him?

38. YES NO   Have to be "pushed" to get an answer to a question?

39. YES NO   Say that he is not sick and doesn't need any treatment?

40. YES NO   Talk about taking his life?

41. YES NO   Report that strange and peculiar ideas come to him?

42. YES NO   Report that he is very much afraid of certain things or people?

43. YES NO   Report that he has ideas of persecution or sinfulness?

44. YES NO   Report that he hears voices that threaten or accuse him?

45. YES NO   Grin or giggle when it is uncalled for?

46. YES NO   Make peculiar expressions with his face?

47. YES NO   Move his body in strange or peculiar ways?

48. YES NO   Use strange words--make up words?

49. YES NO   Repeat over and over certain words or sentences?

50. YES NO   Talk to himself when no one else is around?

51. YES NO   Act as if he is hearing voices?

52. YES NO   Report that voices have said bad things about him?

53. YES NO   Report that voices have said very wonderful things about him?

54. YES NO   Report that voices have threatened to punish or torture him?

55. YES NO Report that voices have ordered him to do certain things?

56. YES NO Say that he actually saw things which couldn't have possibly happened?

57. YES NO Report that he had had peculiar sensations--funny smells or funny tastes?

58. YES NO Believe that some people talk about him or watch him?

59. YES NO Believe that he is being cheated by other people?

60. YES NO Believe that people are plotting against him?

61. YES NO Believe that certain people are controlling his actions?

62. YES NO Believe that things other than people are controlling him?

63. YES NO Believe that he has unusual powers?

64. YES NO Believe that he is evil or sinful?

65. YES NO Believe that familiar things or people have changed or are not real?

66. YES NO Believe that his body is diseased or rotting away?

67. YES NO Believe that he has a direct line to God?

68. YES NO Believe that he is a famous person?

69. YES NO Know where he is?

70. YES NO Know the name of the city and state in which he lives?

71. YES NO Know the names of those around him?

72. YES NO Know the season of the year?

73. YES NO Know the year?

74. YES NO Know his own age?

PATIENT INTERVIEW SCHEDULE

Pt Case No. _____   Pt's Name _____

Date_____   Interviewer _____

1. How does the pt feel that he has been getting along in the last
   four years in terms of his:

   a) Living situation? (where he lives)

   b) His work?

   c) His family relationships?

   d) His illness and his problems as he sees them?

2. What does the pt believe that his troubles are due to? In
   other words why does he think he gets sick?

3. If the pt has been hospitalized since ITC, what reasons does he give for each hospitalization. (Note the approximate date of the hospitalization concerned.)

        <u>Reason</u>   <u>Date</u>

a)

b)

c)

d)

4. What does the pt think would help him the most as far as his doing better is concerned?

5. Does the pt feel that he needs psychiatric care now? Yes____ No____

6. What kind of psychiatric care has helped him the most in the past?

FOR HOME CARE PATIENTS ONLY

7. What did the pt like about ITC?

8. What did the pt dislike about ITC?

9. Would the pt like to be on another ITC program? Yes____ No____

ALL PATIENTS

10. Have the following members of the patient's family had any psychiatric care? (We are concerned with life-time history)

Who (name)	Type Care	Date & Duration of Care
a) Spouse(s) (all)		
_____	_____	_____
_____	_____	_____

Who (name)	Type Care	Date & Duration of Care

b) A father (include step-parents) (If step-relative please state step-father, etc.)

_____   _____   _____
_____   _____   _____

c) A mother (include step-parents)

_____   _____   _____
_____   _____   _____

d) Sisters or brothers (include step-siblings)

_____   _____   _____
_____   _____   _____
_____   _____   _____

AFTER THE INTERVIEW

11. The interviewer is to check the following items which apply to behavior witnessed during the interview on the part of the patient. (Or just prior to the interview.)

Destructive_____ Distractible_____ Impulsive_____ Hostile_____

Irritable_____ Combative_____ Resistive_____ Agitated_____

Talkative_____ Industrious_____ Cheerful_____ Smiling-

Laughing_____ Quiet_____ Reading or occupied doing something

Useful_____ Lacks initiative_____ Brooding_____

Preoccupied_____ Sad_____ Weeping_____ Picks, rubs_____

Anxious_____ Apprehensive_____ Fearful_____ Panicky_____

Suspicious_____ Confused_____ Indifferent_____

Motionless_____ Untidy_____ Suicidal_____ Delusional_____

Hallucinatory_____

12. For the pts known to the interviewer during ITC:
    The interviewer is to give his comments and impression about
    noticeable changes in behavior, appearance, conversation, and
    personality in the patient since ITC.

13. Any other information that may be of value? (Use other side
    as needed)

It is my understanding that the information I give will be kept confidential and will be used by professionals for the purpose of improving the care given to me and to other clients.

Signature_____

Date _____

appendix C

Hospital and Clinic Research Forms

ITC FOLLOW UP

HOSPITAL RECORD DATA

Pt's Name_____   ITC Case Number_____

Study Status_____   Date _____

Hospitalizations Since ITC

(1)

Hospital Name	Admission Data	a) Short Leaves (Days Total) b) Long Leaves (Days Total)	Convalescent Leave or Discharge	Total Days IN
A)_____ _____		a)____ b)_____	_____	_____
B)_____ _____		a)____ b)_____	_____	_____
C)_____ _____		a)____ b)_____	_____	_____
D)_____ _____		a)____ b)_____	_____	_____
E)_____ _____		a)____ b)_____	_____	_____

(2)   Behavior Resulting In Each Admission

(A) _____

_____

B) _____

_____

C) _____

_____

D) _____

_____

E) _____

_____

(3)   Type of Admission

A) _____

B) _____

C) _____

D) _____

E) _____

(4)   Persons Inaugurating the Admission

A) _____

B) _____

C) _____

D) _____

E) _____

(5)   Treatment Received

A) _____

_____

B) _____

_____

C) _____

_____

D) _____

_____

E) _____

_____

(6)   Diagnostic Revisions

A) _____

B) _____

C) _____

D) _____

E) _____

(7)   Treatment for Physical Illnesses

A) _____

B) _____

C) _____

D) _____

E) _____

(8)   Relations with Hospital Staff Members

A) _____

_____

B) _____

_____

C) _____

_____

D) _____

_____

(9)   Symptoms Noted During Hospitalizations
       (Use a for the first hospitalization, b for the second, etc.)

_____ Anxiety   _____ Poor Contact with
                                                 Reality
_____ Depression   _____ Withdrawal

_____ Manic Excitement   _____ Somatic Preoccupa-
                                                 tions
_____ Compulsivity   _____ Motor Control
                                                 Impaired
_____ Obsessions   _____ Disturbed Sensorium

_____ Phobias   _____ Memory Disturbance

_____ Dissociative Episodes   _____ Disoriented

_____ Labile Moods   _____ Conversion Symptoms

_____ Antisocial Behavior   _____ Physiologic Reactions

_____ Paranoid Ideas   _____ Convulsions

_____ Bizarre Ideas   _____ Alcoholism

_____ Bizarre Behavior   _____ Suicidal Behavior

_____ Hallucinations   _____ Homocidal Behavior

_____ Inappropriate Affect   No information available_____

(10)   Relations with Other Patients

A) _____

_____

B) _____

_____

C) _____

_____

D) _____

_____

E) _____

_____

(11)   Any Other Incidents of Note

A) _____

B) _____

C) _____

D) _____

E) _____

(12)   Notes on Pt's Social Environment at Intake

A) _____

B) _____

C) _____

D) _____

E) _____

(13)   Notes on Family – Hospital – Pt. Relationships During
                    Hospitalization

A) _____

B) _____

C) _____

D) _____

E) _____

(14)   Notes on Pt's Social Environment at Discharge

A) _____

B) _____

C) _____

D) _____

E) _____

(15)   Hospital Referral for Continued Treatment

A) _____

B) _____

C) _____

D) _____

E) _____

(16)   Psychiatric Status at Release

A) _____

B) _____

C) _____

D) _____

E) _____

Data Collected By _____

OUTPATIENT CLINIC FORM

Patient's Name _____ Case Number _____

Study Status _____ Date _____

CLINIC	MONTH	STAFF'S NAME	RX CHANGES	OTHER NOTES
		1964		
_____	July	_____	_____	
_____	August	_____	_____	
_____	September	_____	_____	
_____	October	_____	_____	
_____	November	_____	_____	
_____	December	_____	_____	
		1965		
_____	January	_____	_____	
_____	February	_____	_____	
_____	March	_____	_____	
_____	April	_____	_____	
_____	May	_____	_____	
_____	June	_____	_____	
_____	July	_____	_____	
_____	August	_____	_____	
_____	September	_____	_____	
_____	October	_____	_____	
_____	November	_____	_____	
_____	December	_____	_____	

CLINIC	MONTH	STAFF'S NAME	RX CHANGES	OTHER NOTES
		1966		
_____	January	_____	_____	
_____	February	_____	_____	
_____	March	_____	_____	
_____	April	_____	_____	
_____	May	_____	_____	
_____	June	_____	_____	
_____	July	_____	_____	
_____	August	_____	_____	
_____	September	_____	_____	
_____	October	_____	_____	
_____	November	_____	_____	
_____	December	_____	_____	
		1967		
_____	January	_____	_____	
_____	February	_____	_____	
_____	March	_____	_____	
_____	April	_____	_____	
_____	May	_____	_____	
_____	June	_____	_____	
_____	July	_____	_____	
_____	August	_____	_____	
_____	September	_____	_____	
_____	October	_____	_____	
_____	November	_____	_____	
_____	December	_____	_____	

CLINIC	MONTH	STAFF'S NAME	RX CHANGES	OTHER NOTES
		1968		
_____	January	_____	_____	
_____	February	_____	_____	
_____	March	_____	_____	
_____	April	_____	_____	
_____	May	_____	_____	
_____	June	_____	_____	
_____	July	_____	_____	
_____	August	_____	_____	
_____	September	_____	_____	
_____	October	_____	_____	
_____	November	_____	_____	
_____	December	_____	_____	
		1969		
_____	January	_____	_____	
_____	February	_____	_____	
_____	March	_____	_____	
_____	April	_____	_____	
_____	May	_____	_____	
_____	June	_____	_____	
_____	July	_____	_____	
_____	August	_____	_____	

OTHER COMMENTS

appendix D

Tables

TABLE 17

DEMOGRAPHIC CHARACTERISTICS OF STUDY GROUPS ITC
INTAKE (1962) COMPARED TO FOLLOW-UP (1969)
(In Percent)

CHARACTERISTIC	DRUG GROUP		PLACEBO GROUP		CONTROL GROUP	
	1962 N=63	1969 N=57	1962 N=41	1969 N=41	1962 N=48	1969 N=48
Female.	64.9	61.7	68.3	69.9	70.4	69.4
White	68.4	68.1	68.1	66.6	64.8	64.5
Mean age[a]	35.9	42.1	36.2	43.0	37.6	43.4
Education is grade school or less. . . .	12.5	10.6	10.0	8.8	19.2	14.8
High school graduate. .	37.5	36.3	35.0	33.3	13.5	16.7
Married	54.4	38.0	43.9	41.0	51.9	37.1
Never married	24.6	19.0	26.8	20.0	16.7	11.1
In same home for last five years . . .	35.1	37.9	29.3	52.8	19.2	42.0
Socioeconomic status mean score.	60.5	58.7	58.8	63.7	64.9	62.9

[a]In years.

TABLE 18

LIFETIME HOSPITALIZATION EXPERIENCES OF STUDY GROUPS

Hospitalization	Drug Group N=57	Placebo Group N=41	Control Group N=48
Mean times hospitalized (prior ITC).	1.83	2.22	2.28
Mean years hospitalized (prior ITC).	.89	1.09	1.15
Mean times hospitalized (during ITC)	.35[a]	.86	1.39[a]
Mean years hospitalized (during ITC)	.13[a]	.28	.33[a]
Mean times hospitalized (lifetime)	3.37[a]	4.05	5.02[a]
Mean years hospitalized (lifetime)	1.3	1.8	1.8
Percent of lifetime in a hospital.	.03	.04	.04

[a]Differences between these groups were significant at the .05 level and beyond.

TABLE 19

BEHAVIOR PROBLEMS OF PATIENTS REPORTED BY SIGNIFICANT
OTHERS AT FOLLOW-UP (1969)
(In Percent)

Rank	Problem Behaviors of Patients	Total N=146	Drug Group N=57	Placebo Group N=41	Control Group N=48
1	Causes SO a lot of worry	50.0	56.0	35.4[a]	55.2[a]
2	Uncooperative	43.9	45.0	46.2	40.3
3	Talkative and restless	39.0	42.0	38.4	37.3
4	Speaks and behaves oddly	37.1	34.3	36.9	39.8
5	Troublesome at night	34.7	32.0	33.3	39.1
6	Strain due to dependency	30.4	29.8	14.7[a]	39.2[a]
7	Safety causes worry	27.4	23.9	21.8	37.0
8	Requires excessive attention	25.7	23.0[b]	13.4[b]	38.8[b]
9	Upsets household	23.1	24.2	11.4[a]	31.8[a]
10	Excessive physical complaints	22.5	30.7	19.9	21.7
11	A physical strain on SO	22.5	23.3	17.9	25.8
12	Children are ashamed of patient[c]	19.0	11.5	21.0	27.7
13	Causes worry about safety of others	17.6	13.8	15.7	24.0
14	Upsets social life	16.4	19.6	13.4	19.8
15	Sexually rude and improper	16.3	9.1	19.8	22.3
16	Children fear patient[c]	15.8	15.3	26.4	5.5
17	SO fears patient	13.4	8.3	10.9	21.7
18	Causes children's absence from school[c]	9.5	11.5	5.2	11.1
19	SO is ashamed of patient	9.1	10.1	4.2	12.8
20	Causes trouble with the neighbors	9.1	5.8	12.1	9.0

TABLE 19--Continued

Rank	Problem Behaviors of Patients	Total N=146	Drug Group N=57	Placebo Group N=41	Control Group N=48
21	Nursing problem.	7.3	6.4	5.3	13.4
22	Causes absence of others from work.	4.2	6.4	1.8	2.9
	Mean total problem score	...	28.01	26.24	28.77

[a]Differences are significant at the .05 level of confidence and beyond.

[b]Differences are significant at the .01 level of confidence.

[c]The N's for patients with children were: drug group 26, placebo group 19, and control group 18.

TABLE 20

BEHAVIOR PROBLEMS OF PATIENTS REPORTED BY SIGNIFICANT OTHERS AT ITC
INTAKE (1962), SIX MONTHS AFTER INTAKE, AND AT FOLLOW-UP (1969)
(In Percent)

PROBLEM BEHAVIOR OF PATIENTS	DRUG GROUP			PLACEBO GROUP		
	ITC Intake[a] N=44	ITC 6 Months N=54	Follow-Up N=57	ITC Intake[a] N=33	ITC 6 Months N=30	Follow-Up N=41
Causes SO a lot of worry	83.8	34.0	56.3	81.6	55.6	35.2
Uncooperative	48.0	4.1	45.0	39.4	28.6	45.7
Talkative and restless	59.6	8.5	41.9	47.9	33.3	36.7
Speaks and behaves oddly	71.7	8.3	34.2	70.8	32.1	36.7
Troublesome at night	73.4	4.3	32.0	64.2	33.3	32.8
Strain due to dependency	54.3	18.4	29.8	35.8	34.4	14.8
Safety causes worry	51.2	6.3	23.8	49.2	10.7	22.3
Requires excessive attention	55.2	21.3	23.2	36.2	17.9	13.4
Upsets household	60.9	15.2	24.1	41.9	26.9	10.9
Excessive physical complaints	51.0	20.8	30.8	60.0	6.9	19.9
A physical strain on SO	57.0	18.8	23.4	62.5	39.3	18.4
Children fear patient[b]	6.9	6.7	6.2	16.0	11.1	22.2
Causes worry about safety of others	25.4	4.2	25.4	27.4	32.1	27.4
Upsets social life	29.2	18.2	20.3	20.8	19.2	12.9
Sexually rude and improper	33.8	2.1	9.3	26.8	10.7	20.3
Children ashamed of patient[b]	10.9	3.7	5.4	16.8	11.1	9.4
SO fears patient	11.3	2.1	7.8	17.9	13.3	11.0
Causes children's absence from school[b]	37.8	4.5	3.8	19.3	5.6	2.2
SO is ashamed of patient	7.4	2.1	6.8	15.9	6.7	11.0

TABLE 20--Continued

PROBLEM BEHAVIOR OF PATIENTS	DRUG GROUP			PLACEBO GROUP		
	ITC Intake[a] N=44	ITC 6 Months N=54	Follow-Up N=57	ITC Intake[a] N=33	ITC 6 Months N=30	Follow-Up N=41
Causes trouble with neighbors.	15.7	3.1	6.4	17.8	3.6	12.6
Nursing problem.	10.9	...	6.0	18.3	...	5.4
Causes absence of others from work.	36.4	2.6	7.2	21.0	4.8	1.9
Mean total problems score .	33.20	...	28.01	32.80	...	26.24

[a]Not all patients were tested on problem behaviors at ITC intake when the home study first started; this accounts for differentials and increased N's in some cases at follow-up.

[b]N's for patients with children were 26 for the drug group, 19 placebos, and 18 for controls.

TABLE 21

PROBLEM BEHAVIORS OF ALL PATIENTS RANKED AT ITC INTAKE (1962)
AND AT FOLLOW-UP (1969)

PROBLEM BEHAVIOR OF PATIENTS	RANKS		PERCENTS	
	ITC Intake[a] N=120	Follow-up N=146	ITC Intake[a] N=120	Follow-up N=146
Causes SO a lot of worry. . . .	1	1	80.0	50.0
Speaks and behaves oddly. . . .	2	4	71.2	37.1
Troublesome at night.	3	5	68.2	34.7
Talkative and restless.	4	3	59.0	39.0
Excess physical complaints. . .	5	10	57.2	22.5
A physical strain on the SO . .	6	11	57.1	22.7
Upsets household.	7	9	52.0	23.1
Safety causes worry	8	7	50.0	27.4
Uncooperative	9	2	49.0	43.9
Strain due to dependency. . . .	10	6	44.1	30.4
Requires excessive attention. .	11	8	42.2	25.7
Sexually rude and improper. . .	12	15	28.2	16.4
Causes worry about safety of others	13	13	26.2	17.6
Causes absence of others from work	14	22	26.1	4.2
Upsets social life.	15	14	24.0	16.4
Causes children's absence from school[b].	16	18	23.3	9.5
Causes trouble with neighbors	17	20	16.2	9.1
Nursing problem	18	21	14.2	7.3
SO is ashamed of patient. . . .	19	19	14.1	9.1
SO fears patient.	20	17	12.0	13.4
Children ashamed of patient[b]. .	21	12	10.2	19.0
Children fear patient[b].	22	16	10.3	15.8

[a]Not all patients were tested on problem behaviors at ITC intake when the home study first started; this accounts for differentials and increased N's at follow-up.

[b]The N's for patients with children were 55 at intake and 63 at follow-up.

TABLE 22

WOMEN PATIENTS WITH HOMEMAKING DUTIES AT
FOLLOW-UP (1969)
(In Percent)

Homemaking Activity	Drug Group N=35	Placebo Group N=29	Control Group N=34
Primary working role is homemaking	44.4	51.2	42.2
Disabled; incapable of homemaking[a].	14.3	13.2	19.3
Too mentally or physically ill to do housework. . .	9.3	11.4	18.5
Primary homemaker in the household.	42.3	46.9	43.9

[a]Includes both physical and mental disabilities.

TABLE 23

SOCIAL ACTIVITIES OF PATIENTS AT FOLLOW-UP (1969)
(In Percent)

Social Behavior	Drug Group N=57	Placebo Group N=41	Control Group N=48
Has no "good" friends. . . .	48.3	48.6	34.6
Inappropriate upon meeting new persons.	32.8	47.0	38.7
Inappropriate food and table habits	16.7	24.7	19.7
Poor judgments with money. .	32.9	30.5	29.4
Poor grooming habits	16.8	24.0	18.3
Rarely eats with family. . .	13.7	13.0	20.1
Mean social activities score.	19.37	20.86	21.33

TABLE 24

STRESSES AND CLINIC CARE OF FAILURES PRIOR TO HOSPITALIZATIONS
COMPARED WITH SUCCESSES' FIRST SIX MONTHS OF FOLLOW-UP
(In Percent)

VARIABLES	SUCCESSES First Six Months[a] of Follow-Up N=51	FAILURES Three Months Prior[a] to Hospitalizations N=75
Clinic Care		
Regular attendance	34.3	20.2
Sporadic attendance. . . .	16.4	25.3
Taking regular stable dose of medication . . .	31.4	2.2
Stresses		
Intrapsychic	16.2	36.4
Interpersonal.	26.9	18.3
Physical	7.4	7.9
Social structural (economic hardship, job losses). . . .	8.1	8.9
Combination of two or more stresses.	10.4	17.3
No stress evident.	13.0	0.0

[a]The reader is advised to note that these time periods differ; no period of prehospitalization was available for successes.

TABLE 25

VOCATIONAL PERFORMANCE OF SUCCESSES AND FAILURES
(In Percent)

Vocational Performance	Successes N=24	Failures N=23
Patient has a vocation	62.0	64.0
Occupational level had dropped after ITC (1964-1969).	36.7	26.4
Continuity of work history after ITC (1964-1969).	32.2	25.4
Main breadwinner is other than patient or spouse.	12.5	26.4[a]
Patient is main breadwinner.	58.3	42.6
Patient's dependency on others increased after ITC (1964-1969).	13.2	14.0

[a]Statistically significant at the .05 level.

TABLE 26

ECONOMIC FACTORS COMPARED FOR SUCCESSES AND FAILURES
(In Percent)

Economic Variable	Successes N=24	Failures N=23
Mean socioeconomic status score.	62.0	64.0
Socioeconomic status worsened after ITC (1964-1969).	23.0	18.2
High school graduate	34.8	27.2
Person upon whom patient is economically dependent, changed after ITC (1964-1969).	18.7	32.2
Yearly income $3,500 or less	55.4	65.3[a]
Annual income in home $5,000 or less . . .	56.2	81.3[a]

[a]Approaches statistical significance at the .10 level.

TABLE 27

DOMESTIC AND PARENTAL ROLES OF SUCCESSES
COMPARED WITH FAILURES
(In Percent)

Domestic Role	Successes N=35	Failures N=63
Over 50 percent of time spent in homemaking	68.4	75.3
Too mentally or physically ill to do housework.	19.1	17.0
Works outside of home.	18.3	8.4
Someone else available to do housework . .	5.9	15.2
Acceptance of responsibility as a parent is poor or nil[b]	13.0	30.2[a]
Parental abilities worsened after ITC[b] (1964-1969).	20.3	30.1

[a]Statistically significant at the .01 level.

[b]N's for women patients with children were: successes (15) and failures (20).

TABLE 28

DOMESTIC TASKS PERFORMED WITHOUT ASSISTANCE BY
SUCCESSES COMPARED WITH FAILURES
(In Percent)

Domestic Task	Successes N=35	Failures N=63
Cleaning house	80.8	72.0
Grocery shopping	85.3	63.4
Other shopping	96.3	76.4
Cooking meals.	73.4	67.2
Laundry and cleaning	75.5	69.3
Budgeting and paying bills	77.9	46.1[a]
Planning daily activities.	99.4	89.3
Solving daily problems	98.3	68.4[a]
Total domestic performance mean score. . . .	19.03	17.80[b]
Total domestic score has worsened since ITC intake (1962-1969)	15.3	25.0[b]

[a]Statistically significant at the .05 level.

[b]Approaches statistical significance at the .10 level.

TABLE 29

SOCIAL ACTIVITIES OF SUCCESSES COMPARED WITH FAILURES
(In Percent)

Social Activity	Successes N=61	Failures N=85
Trouble with friendships	40.2	52.4[a]
Friendship pattern worsened after ITC (1964-1969).	42.1	44.4
Poor social adjustment	43.4	47.3
Mean social participation score.	23.27	22.93

[a]Approaches statistical significance at .10 level.

TABLE 30

HETEROSEXUAL RELATIONSHIPS OF SUCCESSES
COMPARED WITH FAILURES
(In Percent)

Heterosexual Relationships	Successes N=61	Failures N=85
Mean number of marriages	1.2	1.3
Never married.	13.3	21.0
Married at follow-up (1969).	50.1	33.2[a]
Change in marital status since ITC (1964-1969).	10.2	17.3[b]
Relationship with opposite sex is pathological (as described by SO)	35.3	58.1[b]
Change in relational ties since ITC is due to patient's pathology	16.4	30.2[b]

[a]Statistically significant at the .05 level.

[b]Approaches statistical significance at the .10 level.

TABLE 31

LIVING ARRANGEMENTS OF SUCCESSES COMPARED WITH FAILURES
(In Percent)

Residential Variable	Successes N=61	Failures N=85
Residential Mobility (1964 to 1969)		
Mean Residential Moves	1.2	1.4
Household moves due to patients' intrapsychic problems.	13.1	33.0[a]
Household moves due to necessities or for personal improvements	36.6	19.9
Patients' Living Arrangements at Follow-Up, 1969		
Alone.	4.8	17.2
With spouse.	50.1	32.9
With parent.	20.4	19.4
With others.	23.4	29.2

[a]Statistically significant at .01 level.

Bibliography

Albee, George. "Through the Looking Glass." *International Journal of Psychiatry* 9 (1970–71):293–98.

Albini, Joseph. "The Role of the Social Worker in an Experimental Community Mental Health Clinic: Experiences and Future Implications." *Community Mental Health Journal* 14, no. 2 (April 1968): 111–19.

American Medical Association. "Queries Regarding Schizophrenia: Recent Findings in Sex Chromosomal Anomalies." *Journal of the American Medical Association* 183, no. 12 (March 1963):1033–34.

Angrist, Shirley S.; Lefton, Mark; Dinitz, Simon; and Pasamanick, Benjamin. *Women After Treatment: A Study of Former Mental Patients and Their Normal Neighbors.* New York: Appleton-Century-Crofts, 1968.

———; Dinitz, Simon; Lefton, Mark; and Pasamanick, Benjamin. "The Unmarried Woman after Psychiatric Treatment." *Mental Hygiene* 51, no. 2 (April 1967).

———; Lefton, Mark; Dinitz, Simon; and Pasamanick, Benjamin. "Tolerance of Deviant Behavior, Posthospital Performance Levels, and Rehospitalization." *Proceedings of the Third World Congress of Psychiatry.*

Anthony, James, and Benedek, Therese. *Parenthood: Its Psychology and Psychopathology.* Boston: Little Brown and Company, Inc., 1970.

Artiss, Keneth, ed. *The Symptom as Communication in Schizophrenia*. New York: Grune and Stratton, 1959.

Beck, Samuel J. "Families of Schizophrenic and of Welfare Children: Method, Concepts, and Some Results." *American Journal of Orthopsychiatry* 30 (1960):247–61.

Bell, Norman W. "Extended Family Relations of Disturbed and Well Families." In *The Psychosocial Interior of the Family*, edited by Gerald Handel. Chicago: Aldine Publishing Company, 1967.

Bellak, L., ed. *Schizophrenia: A Review of the Syndrome*. New York: Logos Press, 1958.

Bentz, W. Kenneth, and Edgerton, J. Wilbert. "Consensus on Attitudes toward Mental Illness." *Archives of General Psychiatry* 22 (May 1970):468–72.

Bergen, John R. "Biologic Concomitants of Schizophrenia." *Mental Hygiene* 50 (1966):505

Bindman, Arthur J., and Spiegel, Allen D., eds. *Perspectives in Community Health*. Chicago: Aldine Publishing Company, 1969.

Block, Jeanne. "Parents of Schizophrenic, Neurotic, Asthmatic, and Congenitially Ill Children: A Comparative Study." *Archives of General Psychiatry* 20 (June 1969):659–74.

Blum, Gerald S. *Psychoanalytic Theories of Personality*. New York: McGraw Hill Book Company, 1953.

Broen, William E., Jr. *Schizophrenia Research and Theory*. New York: Academic Press, 1968.

Brown, George W. "Experiences of Discharged Chronic Schizophrenic Patients in Various Types of Living Groups." *Millbank Fund Quarterly* 37 (1959):105–31.

———; Carstairs, G. Morris; and Topping, Gillian T. "Post Hospital Adjustment of Chronic Mental Patients." *Lancet*, September 1959, pp. 685–89.

Bryce, Forbes; Halerud, George; Mitchell, Gary; Weinstein, Alan; and Newswander, Donald. "Problems in Prediction of a Schizophrenic Population." *Archives of General Psychiatry* 15, no. 2 (August 1966):140–43.

Buss, Arnold H., and Buss, Edith H., eds. *Theories of Schizophrenia*. New York: Atherton Press, 1969.

Caffey, Eugene, Jr., M.D.; Hollister, Leo H., M.D.; Kaim, Samuel C.,

M.D.; and Pokorny, Alex D., M.D. "Drug Treatment in Psychiatry," *International Journal of Psychiatry* 9 (1970):428–71.

———; Diamond, L. S.; Frank, T. V.; Grasberger, J. C.; Herman, L.; Klett, C. J.; and Rothstein, C. "Discontinuation or Reduction of Chemotherapy in Chronic Schizophrenics." *Journal of Chronic Disorders* 17 (1964).

Cancro, Robert, ed. *The Schizophrenic Reactions: A Critique of the Concept, Hospital Treatment, and Current Research.* New York: Brunner/Mazel Publishers, 1970.

Caplan, Gerald. *A Community Approach to Preventive Psychiatry.* New York: Grune and Stratton, Inc., 1961.

Carstairs, G. M. "The Social Limits of Eccentricity: An English Study." In *Culture and Mental Health*, edited by Marvin K. Opler. New York: MacMillan Publishers, 1959.

Cumming, Elaine, and Cumming, John. *Closed Ranks: An Experiment in Mental Health Education.* Cambridge, Mass.: Harvard University Press, 1957.

Cumming, John, and Cumming, Elaine. *Ego and Milieu.* New York: Basic Books, Inc., 1967.

Davis, James A. *Education for Positive Mental Health.* Chicago: Aldine Publishing Company, 1965.

Denzin, Norman K., and Spitzer, Stephan. "Paths to the Mental Hospital and Staff Predictions of Patient Role Behavior." *Journal of Health and Human Behavior* 7 (1966):265–71.

Deykin, Eva; Klerman, Gerald; and Armor, David. "The Relative of Schizophrenic Patients: Clinical Judgements of Potential Emotional Resourcefulness." *American Journal of Orthopsychiatry* 36, no. 3 (April 1966): 518–28.

Dightman, Cameron, and Marks, John. "Employer Attitudes Toward the Employment of the Ex-Psychiatric Patient." *Mental Hygiene*, October 1968, p. 562.

Dinitz, Simon. "Policy Implications of an Experimental Study in the Home Care of Schizophrenics." *Sociological Focus* 1, no. 2 (Winter 1967):1–20.

———; Angrist, Shirley; Lefton, Mark; Pasamanick, Benjamin. "The Posthospital Psychological Functioning of Former Mental Hospital Patients." *Mental Hygiene* 45, no. 4 (October 1961):579–88.

———; Lefton, Mark; Angrist, Shirley; and Pasamanick, Benjamin.

"Psychiatric and Social Attributes as Predictors of Case Outcome in Mental Hospitalization." *Social Problems* 8, no. 4 (Spring 1961).

———; Lefton, Mark; and Pasamanick, Benjamin. "Status Perceptions in a Mental Hospital." *Social Forces* 38, no. 2 (December 1959).

———; Lefton, Mark; Simpson, Jon E.; Patterson, Ralph M., and Pasamanick, Benjamin. "Correlates and Consequences of Patient Interaction and Isolation in a Mental Hospital." *The Journal of Nervous and Mental Disease* 126, no. 5 (November 1958).

———;Lefton, Mark; Simpson Jon E.; Pasamanick, Benjamin; and Patterson, Ralph M. "The Ward Behavior of Psychiatric Patients." *Social Problems* 6, no. 2 (Fall 1958).

———; Mangus, A. R., and Pasamanick, Benjamin. "Integration and Conflict in Self-Other Conceptions as Factors in Mental Illness." *Sociometry* 22 (March 1959).

———; Pasamanick, Benjamin; Albini, Joseph L.; Scarpitti, Frank R.; and Lefton, Mark. "Home Care for Schizophrenic Patients: A Controlled Study." *The British Journal of Social Psychiatry* 1, no. 4 (1967).

———; Scarpitti, Frank; Albini, Joseph L.; Lefton, Mark; and Pasamanick, Benjamin. "An Experimental Study in the Prevention of Hospitalization of Schizophrenics: Thirty Months of Experience." *American Journal of Orthopsychiatry* 35, no. 1 (January 1965).

Dunham, Warren H. "Social Class and Schizophrenia." *American Journal of Orthopsychiatry* 34, No. 4 (July 1964):78–84.

———., and Faris, Robert. *Mental Disorders in Urban Areas.* Chicago: The University of Chicago Press, 1939.

Elard, Donald M.; Brooks, George W.; Diane, William; and Taylor, Marjorie B. "The Rehabilitation of the Hospitalized Mentally Ill— The Vermont Story." *American Journal of Public Health* 52 (January–June 1962):165–78.

Englehardt, David M., and Freedman, Norbert. "Maintenance Drug Therapy: The Schizophrenic in the Community." In *Social Psychiatry*, edited by Ari Kiev, M.D. New York: Science House, 1969.

Evera, Paul; Davenport, Pearl; and Decker, Lila. "Pre-Intake Dropout in a Psychiatric Clinic." *Mental Hygiene* 49 (1965):558–68.

Fiensilver, David. "Communication in Families of Schizophrenic Patients." *Archives of General Psychiatry* 22 (February 1970): 143–48.

Flekkoy, K.; Astrup, C.; and Hartman, T. "Word Association in Schizophrenics: A Ten-Year Follow Up," *Acta Psychiatrica Scandanavica* 45 (1969):209–16.

Flomenhoft, Kalman; Kaplan, David M.; and Langsley, Donald. "Avoiding Psychiatric Hospitalization." *Social Work* 14, no. 4 (October 1969):38–45.

Freeman, Howard E. "Attitudes toward Mental Illness among Relatives of Former Patients." *American Sociological Review* 26 (1961), p. 59.

———, and Simmons, Ozzie G. *The Mental Patient Comes Home.* New York: John Wiley and Sons, 1963.

———. "Mental Patients in the Community: Family Settings and Performance Levels." *American Sociological Review* 23 (1958): 147–54.

———. "The Use of the Survey in Mental Illness." *Mental Hygiene* 44, no. 3 (July 1960):401–4.

Fuller, R. G. "Expectation of Hospital Life and Outcome for Mental Patients on First Admission." *Psychiatric Quarterly* 4 (1930): 295–323.

Goffman, Erving. *Asylums.* New York: Anchor Books, 1961.

———. *Stigma.* Englewood Cliffs, N. J.: Prentice Hall, Inc., 1963.

Goldfarb, William. "The Mutual Impact of Mother and Child in Childhood Schizophrenia." *American Journal of Orthopsychiatry* 31 (October 1961): 738–47.

Gordon, Hiram; Rosenberg, David; and Morris, William. "Leisure Activity of Schizophrenic Patients after Return to the Community." *Mental Hygiene* 50 (1966):452–58.

Gorman, Michael. "The Public Arena." *International Journal of Psychiatry* 9 (1970):299–302.

Gottheil, Edward; Paredes, Alfonso; Exline, Ralph; and Winkelmayer, Richard. "Communication of Affect in Schizophrenia." *Archives of General Psychiatry* 22 (May 1970):439–44.

Gotheil, Joseph. "Age, Appearance, and Schizophrenia." *Archives of General Psychiatry* 19, no. 2 (August 1968), p. 232.

Gove, Walter R. "Societal Reaction as an Explanation of Mental Illness: An Evaluation." *American Sociological Review* 35 (October 1970):873–84.

Gralnick, Alexander, ed. *The Psychiatric Hospital as a Therapeutic Instrument.* New York: Brunner Mazel Publishers, 1969.

Grinker, Roy R. "An Essay on Schizophrenia and Science." *Archives of General Psychiatry* 20 (January 1969):1–24.

Guntrip, Harry. *Schizoid Phenomena Object-Relations and the Self.* New York: International Universities Press Inc., 1969.

Haley, Jay. "The Family of the Schizophrenic: A Model System." In *The Psychosocial Interior of the Family,* edited by Gerald Handel. Chicago: Aldine Publishing Company, 1967.

Hanson, Philip G.; Rolhaus, Paul; Cleveland, Sidney; Johnson, Dale L.; and McCall, Daniel. "Employment after Psychiatric Hospitalization: An Orientation for Texas Employment Personnel." *Mental Hygiene* 48, no. 1 (January 1964), p. 676.

Harrow, Martin; Tucker, Gary J.; and Bromet, Evelyn. "Short Term Prognosis of Schizophrenic Patients." *Archives of General Psychiatry* 21 (1969):195–202.

Havens, Leston. "Anatomy of Schizophrenia." *Journal of the American Medical Association* 196, no. 4 (April 1966):328–31.

Henry, Jules. "My Life with Families of Psychotic Children." In *The Psychosocial Interior of the Family,* edited by Gerald Handel. Chicago: Aldine Publishing Company, 1967.

Hollingshead, August B., "Two Factor Index of Social Position," New Haven, Connecticut, 1957 (privately printed).

———, and Redlich, Frederick C. *Social Class and Mental Illness.* New York: John Wiley and Sons, Inc., 1958.

———, and Duff, Raymond S. *Sickness and Society.* New York: Harper and Row, 1968.

Jackson, Don D., ed. *Communication, Family, and Marriage: Human Communication Volume I.* Palo Alto, California: Science and Behavior Books, 1968.

———, ed. *Therapy, Communication, and Change: Human Communication Volume II.* Palo Alto, California: Science and Behavior Books, 1968.

———, ed. *The Etiology of Schizophrenia.* New York: Basic Books, Inc., 1960.

Joint Commission on Mental Illness and Health. *Action for Mental Health.* New York: John Wiley and Sons, Inc., 1961.

Kadushin, Charles. *Why People Go to Psychiatrists*. New York: Atherton Press, 1969.

Kallman, Franz J., ed. *Expanding Goals of Genetics in Psychiatry*. New York: Grune and Stratton, 1963.

Kamer, M. *Application of Life Table Methodology to the Study of Mental Hospital Populations*. Washington, D.C.: American Psychiatric Association, 1956.

Kamman, G. R. "A Critical Evaluation of a Total Push Program for Regressed Schizophrenics in a State Hospital." *Psychiatric Quarterly* 28 (1954):650–67.

Kantor, Robert E. "Implications of Process-Reactive Schizophrenia for Rehabilitation." *Mental Hygiene* 48, no. 4 (October 1964), p. 644.

———; "Schizophrenia-The Protestant Ethic." *Mental Hygiene* 50 (1966), p. 18.

Kaplan, Gerald. *Principles of Preventive Psychiatry*. New York: Basic Books, Inc., 1964.

Kramel, Madeline. "Total Institutions and Self Mortification." *Journal of Health and Social Behavior* 10, no. 2 (June 1969):134–41.

Keith, C. "Multiple Transfers of Psychotherapy Patients." *Archives of General Psychiatry* 14 (February 1966):185–89.

Kelley, Francis E. "Research in Schizophrenia—Implications for Social Workers." *Social Work* 10 no. 1 (January 1965):32–44.

Kind, Hans. "The Psychogenesis of Schizophrenia—A Review of the Literature," *The International Journal of Psychiatry* 3 (1967):383–403.

Klein, Rachel Gittelman, and Klein, Donald F. "Premorbid Adjustment and Prognosis in Schizophrenia," *Journal of Psyciatric Research* 7 (1969):35–53.

Kleiner, Robert J., and Parker, Seymour. "Goal Striving, Social States, and Mental Disorder: A Research Review." *American Sociological Review* 28 (1963), p. 200.

Kolb, Lawrence C. "Community Mental Health Centers." *The International Journal of Psychiatry* 9 (1970–71):283–92.

Kursch, Theodore, and Nikelly, Arthur. "The Schizophrenic in College." *Archives of General Psychiatry* 15 (July 1966):54–58.

Labrachi, Gary; Turner, A. Jay; and Zabo, Lawrence J. "Social Class and Participation in Out Patient Care by Schizophrenics." *Community Mental Health Journal* 2 (1969):394–402.

Langer, Jonas. *Theories of Development.* New York: Holt, Rinehart, and Winston, Inc., 1969.

Langner, Thomas S., and Michael, Stanley T. *Life Stress and Mental Health: The Midtown Manhattan Study.* New York: Free Press of Glencoe, 1963.

Langsley, Donald, and Kaplan, David. *The Treatment of Families in Crisis.* New York: Grune and Stratton, 1968.

Lanua, Victor. "The Etiology and Epidemiology of Mental Illness and Problems of Methodology with Special Emphasis on Schizophrenia." *Mental Hygiene* 47, no. 4 (October 1963):617–21.

Lee, H. *Two Rehabilitation Programs for the Chronic Services.* Final Project Report, Medfield State Hospital Project, Grant OM-547, Harding, Mass. September 1961–August 1964.

Lefton, Mark; Angrist, Shirley; Dinitz, Simon; and Pasamanick, Benjamin. "Social Class, Expectations, and Performance of Mental Patients." *The American Journal of Sociology* 68, no. 1 (July 1962).

———; Dinitz, Simon; Angrist, Shirley; and Pasamanick, Benjamin. "Former Mental Health Patients and Their Neighbors—A Comparison of Performance Levels." *Journal of Health and Human Behavior,* Summer 1966, pp. 106–13.

Lehrman, N. S. "A State Hospital Population Five Years after Admission: A Yardstick for Evaluative Comparison of Follow-Up Studies." *Psychiatric Quarterly* 34 (1960):365–73.

Leighton, Alexander H.; Clausen, John A.; and Wilson, Robert N., eds. *Exploration in Social Psychiatry.* New York: Basic Books, Inc., 1957.

Lorr, Maurice; Klett, James C.; Mc Nair, Douglas M.; Lasky, Julian. *Inpatient Multidimensional Psychiatric Scale* (IMPS) *Manual.* Veterans Administration, 1962.

Lucas, Leon. "Family Influences and Schizophrenic Reaction." *American Journal of Orthopsychiatry* 34 (April 1964):527–35.

Ludwig, A. M., and Marx, A. J. "Influencing Techniques of Chronic Schizophrenics." *Archives of General Psychiatry* 18, no. 6 (June 1968):681–89.

May, Philip R. *Treatment of Schizophrenia.* New York: Science House, Inc., 1968.

Mandelbrote, B. M. and Trick, K. L. K. "Social and Clinical Factors in the Outcome of Schizophrenia." *Acta Psychiatrica Scandanavica* 46 (1970):24–34.

Mechanic, David. *Mental Health and Social Policy.* Englewood Cliffs, N. J.: Prentice-Hall, Inc., 1969.

Meltzoff, Julian, and Kornreich, Melvin. *Research in Psychotherapy.* New York: Atherton Press, Inc., 1970.

Menael, W. M., and Rapport, S. "Outpatient Treatment for Chronic Schizophrenic Patients." *Archives of General Psychiatry* 8 (February 1963):193–96.

Menninger, Karl. *Theory of Psychoanalytic Technique.* New York: Basic Books, Inc., 1958.

Meyers, Donald, and Goldfarb, William. "Studies of Perplexity in Mothers of Schizophrenic Children." *American Journal of Orthopsychiatry* 31 (July 1961):551–64.

Michaux, William W.; Katz, Martin M.; Kurland, Albert A.; and Gansereit, Kathleen H. *The First Year Out: Mental Patients after Hospitalization.* Baltimore: The Johns Hopkins Press, 1969.

Midnick, Sarnoff. "A Longitudinal Study of Children with a High Risk for Schizophrenia." *Mental Hygiene* 50 (1966):523–28.

Miller, Dorothy. *Worlds That Fail, Part I: Retrospective Analysis of Mental Patients' Careers.* Research Monograph, no. 6. State of California: Department of Mental Hygiene, 1965.

———, and Dawson, William. *Worlds That Fail, Part II: Disbanded Worlds: A Study of Returns to the Mental Hospital.* Research Monograph, no. 7. State of California: Department of Mental Hygiene, 1965.

———, and Dawson, William. "Effects of Stigma on Re-Employment of Ex-Mental Patients." *Mental Hygiene* 49 (1969), p. 281.

Miller, Leo. "Family Structure and Conditions of Hospitalization for Schizophrenia." *Community Mental Health Journal* 3, no. 2 (1967): 125–31.

Mishler, Elliot. "Families and Schizophrenia: An Experimental Study." *Mental Hygiene* 50 (1966), p. 552.

———, and Scotch, Norman A. "Sociocultural Factors in the Epidemiology of Schizophrenia." *International Journal of Psychiatry* 1 (1965):258–98.

———, and Waxler, Nancy E. *Interaction in Families: An Experimental Study of Family Processes and Schizophrenia.* New York: John Wiley and Sons, Inc., 1968.

Molholm, Lois. "Female Patients and Normal Female Controls: A Restudy Ten Years Later." Ph.D. dissertation, The Ohio State University, 1970.

Morgan, Donald, and Hedlund, James. "Schizophrenic Symptom Change with Rehospitalization." *Archives of General Psychiatry* 19, no. 2 (August 1968), p. 227.

Morris, William E.; Gordon, Hiram L.; and Rosenberg, David. "Recreation, Energy Level, and Work of Schizophrenics." *Mental Hygiene* 49 (April 1965):172–81.

Morrissy, James R. "The Case for Family Care of the Mentally Ill." *Community Mental Health Journal*, Monograph, no. 2. New York: Behavioral Publications, Inc., 1967.

Murphy, H. B. M.; Wittkower, Ed.; Fried, J.; and Ellenberger, H. "A Cross-Cultural Survey of Schizophrenic Symptomatology." *International Journal of Social Psychiatry* 9 (1963):237–49.

Murphy, Jane M., and Leighton, Alexander H., eds. *Approaches to Cross Cultural Psychiatry.* Ithaca, New York: Cornell University Press, 1965.

Myers, Jerome K., and Bean, Lee L. *A Decade Later: A Follow-Up of Social Class and Mental Illness.* New York: John Wiley and Sons, Inc., 1968.

Myers, Jerome K., and Roberts, Bertram H. *Family and Class Dynamics in Mental Illness.* New York: John Wiley and Sons, Inc., 1964.

Nuttall, Ronald L., and Solomon, Leonard F. "Prognosis in Schizophrenia: The Role of Premorbid, Social Class, and Demographic Factors." *Behavioral Science* 15 (May 1970):255–64.

Offord, David R., and Cross, Lucien A. "Behavioral Antecedents of Adult Schizophrenia." *Archives of General Psychiatry* 21 (September 1969):267–83.

Olshansky, Simon; Grob, Samuel; and Ekdahl, Miriam. "Survey of Employment Experiences of Patients Discharged." *Mental Hygiene* 44, no. 3 (October 1960):511–18.

Orlinsky, N., and D'Elia, E. "Rehospitalization of the Schizophrenic

Patient." *Archives of General Psychiatry* 10 (January 1964): 47–54.

Pasamanick, Benjamin; Scarpitti, Frank R.; Lefton, Mark; Dinitz, Simon; Wernert, John J.; and McPheeters, Harold. "Home vs. Hospital Care for Schizophrenics." *The Journal of the American Medical Association* 187 (January 1964):177–81.

———; Scarpitti, Frank R.; and Dinitz, Simon. *Schizophrenics in the Community.* New York: Appleton-Century-Crofts, 1967.

Plank, Robert. "Are We Treating All Schizophrenics?" *American Journal of Orthopsychiatry* 35, no. 4 (July 1965):793–94.

Plog, Stanley C., and Edgerton, Robert B., eds. *Changing Perspectives in Mental Illness.* New York: Holt, Rinehart, and Winston, Inc., 1969.

Pollak, Max; Woerner, Margaret G.; Goldberg, Philip; and Klein, Donald. "Siblings of Schizophrenic and Non Schizophrenic Psychiatric Patients." *Archives of General Psychiatry* 20 (June 1969): 658–59.

Prien, Robert, and Cole, Jonathan. "High Dose Chlorpromazine Therapy in Chronic Schizophrenia." *Report of the National Institute of Mental Health—Psychopharmachology Research Branch Collaboration Study Group.*

Rabken, Richard. "Shall We Burn Thomas Szasz at the Stake?" *Psychiatry and Social Science Review* 4, no. 8 (June 1970):6–11.

Raphael, Theophile, and Raphael, Louise. "Genes and Schizophrenia." *Journal of the American Medical Association* 180, no. 3 (April 1962):215–19.

Rasken, Marjorie, and Dyson, William. "Treatment Problems Leading to Readmissions of Schizophrenic Patients." *Archives of General Psychiatry* 19, no. 3 (September 1968):174–82.

Ricks, David, and Namechi, Gene. "Symbiosis, Sacrifice, and Schizophrenia." *Mental Hygiene* 50 (1966):541–46.

Ring, Stephen L., and Schein, Lawrence. "Attitudes Toward Mental Illness and the Use of Caretakers in a Black Community." *The American Journal of Orthopsychiatry* 40 (July 1970):710–17.

Robins, Lee N. *Deviant Children Grown Up.* Baltimore: Williams and Williams Company, 1966.

Rosen, George. *Madness in Society.* New York: Harper and Row, 1968.

Rosenbaum, C. Peter. *The Meaning of Madness.* New York: Science House, 1970.

Rosenthal, Alan; Behrens, Manfred I.; and Chodoff, Paul. "Communication in Lower Class Families of Schizophrenics—Methodological Problems." *Archives of General Psychiatry* 18 (April 1968):464–70.

Rosenthal, David. "Problems of Sampling and Diagnosis in the Major Twin Studies of Schizophrenia." *Schizophrenia Bulletin,* December 1969. National Clearing House for Mental Health Information. Bethesda, Maryland: National Institute of Mental Health.

Rushing, William A. "Two Patterns in the Relationship between Social Class and Mental Hospitalization." *American Sociological Review* 34 (August 1969):533–41.

Ryper, Paul E. "The Etiology of Schizophrenia with Reference to the Double Bind and the Moore-Anderson Conceptualization of Symbolic Interaction." *Hueristics* 1, no. 21 (December 1969): 18–36.

Sampson, Harold; Messinger, Sheldon L.; and Towne, Robert D. *Schizophrenic Women: Studies in Marital Crisis.* New York: Atherton Press, 1964.

Sanders, Richard; Smith, Robert S.; and Weinman, Bernard S. *Chronic Psychoses and Recovery.* San Francisco: Jossey-Bass, Inc., 1967.

Scheff, Thomas J., ed. *Mental Illness and Social Processes.* New York: Harper and Row, 1967.

———. *Being Mentally Ill—A Sociological Theory.* Chicago: Aldine Publishing Company, 1966.

———. "Societal Reactions to Deviance: Ascriptive Elements in the Psychiatric Screening of Mental Patients." *Social Problems* 11 (1964):401–13.

Schwartz, Charlotte. "Perspective on Deviance: Wives' Definitions of Their Husbands' Mental Illness." *Psychiatry* 20 (June 1969): 618–42.

Shore, Milton F., and Mannino, Fortune V., eds. *Mental Health and the Community—Problems, Programs, and Strategies.* New York: Behavioral Publications, 1969.

Siegler, Miriam; Osmond, Humphrey; and Mann, Harriet. "Laing's Models of Madness." *Psychiatry and Social Science Review* 4, no. 1 (January 1970):3–18.

Simmons, Ozzie G., and Freeman, Howard E. "Familial Expectations and Post Hospital Performance of Mental Patients." *Human Relations*, August 1959, pp. 233–41.

Spitzer, Stephan, and Denzin, Norman K., eds. *The Mental Patient: Studies in the Sociology of Deviance.* New York: McGraw Hill, 1968.

Srole, Leo; Langner, Thomas S.; Opler, Marvin K.; and Rennie, Thomas. *Mental Health in the Metropolis: The Midtown Manhattan Study Volume I.* New York: McGraw Hill Book Company, Inc., 1962.

Stabenau, James. "Heredity and Environment in Schizophrenia—The Contribution of Twin Studies." *Archives of General Psychiatry* 18 (April 1968):458–63.

Stein, Helen. "Reflections on Schizoid Phenomena." *Psychiatry and Social Science Review* 4, no. 12 (October 1970):12–28.

Stierlen, Helm. *Conflict and Reconciliation.* New York: Science House, 1969.

Stone, Michael H. "Schizophrenia—The Evolution of a Concept." *Psychiatry and Social Science Review* 4, no. 12 (October 1970): 12–16.

Stotland, Ezra. *The Psychology of Hope.* San Francisco: Jossey-Bass, Inc., 1969.

Strupp, Hans; Fox, Ronald; and Lessler, Ken. *Patients View Their Psychotherapy.* Baltimore: The Johns Hopkins Press, 1969.

Sullivan, Harry Stack. *Schizophrenia as a Human Process.* New York: W. W. Norton and Company, Inc., 1962.

Szasz, Thomas S. *Law, Liberty, and Psychiatry.* New York: The MacMillan Company, 1963.

———. "The Myth of Mental Illness." *The American Psychologist* 15 (February 1960):113–18.

Turner, R. Jay, and Wagenfeld, Morton O. "Occupational Mobility and Schizophrenia: An Assessment of the Social Causation and Social Selection Hypothesis." *American Sociological Review* 32, no. 1 (February 1967):104–13.

Valliant, George E. "Unraveling Schizophrenia or Twenty Years of Toil on a Gordian Knot." *Psychiatry and Social Science Review* 3 (November 1969):16–23.

Veterans Administration Hospital Psychiatric Evaluation Project. *Pattern of Mental Patient Post-Hospital Adjustment.* International Report 65, no. 1 (February 1965), Washington, D.C.

———. *Release and Community Stay Criteria in Evaluating Psychiatric Treatment. International Report* 63, no. 3 (March 1963), Washington, D.C.

Waring, Mary L. "Averting Hospitalization for Adult Schizophrenia —A Search for Ameliorative Factors." *Social Work* 11, no. 4 (October 1966):34–42.

Watl, N. F.; Stolorow, R. D.; Lubinsky, Amy W.; and McClelland, D. C. "School Adjustment and Behavior of Children Hospitalized for Schizophrenia as Adults." *American Journal of Orthopsychiatry* 40, no. 4 (July 1970):637–57.

Weinberg, S. Kirson, ed. *The Sociology of Mental Disorders.* Chicago: Aldine Publishing Company, 1967.

Williams, Richard H., and Ozarin, Lucy D., eds. *Community Mental Health—An International Perspective.* San Francisco: Jossey Bass, Inc., 1968.

Wilson, Donald P.; Knapp, Sarah; Dondis, Ernest; and Chadbourne, Mary. "Outpatient Screening of Hospital Candidates." *Mental Hygiene* 49 (1965), p. 364.

Winkelman, N. M., Jr. "A Clinical and Sociocultural Study of 200 Psychiatric Patients Started on Chloropromazine 10 1/2 Years Ago," *American Journal of Psychiatry* 120:861–69.

Zigler, E., and Phillips, L. "Social Competence and Outcome in Psychiatric Disorders." *Journal of Abnormal Psychology* 63 (September 1961):264–71.

Zolnick, Edwin S., and Lantz, Edna M. "A Comparative Study of Return Rates to Two Mental Hospitals." *Community Mental Health Journal,* Fall 1965, pp.233–37.

Index